Kid Talk

Kid Talk

A Faith-Based Curriculum for Grieving Children

With

Our Story: Memory Book

MEL ERICKSON

Copyright Information
Kid Talk Curriculum A Faith-Based Curriculum for Grieving Children
&
Our Story: Memory Book
Copyright © 2021 Mel Erickson.

Please respect my work.

Mel Erickson

For inquiries, sales or permissions requests, please contact the publisher: Mel Erickson.

www.kidtalkgrief.com or mel@kidtalkgrief.com

Scripture Quotations are from:

Printed in the United States of America by Amazon KDP.
First Edition - 2021.

ISBN – 978-1-7365868-0-8

www.kidtalkgrief.com

Contents 1

Contents 2

Contents 3

To all the bereaved children in my life –
past, present, and future -

Mel Erickson

Acknowledgments

Kid Talk would not exist were it not for the parents who had the wisdom to seek support for their grieving children while absorbed in grief themselves. Thank you parents, for being alert to your child's needs. You were brave enough to enter the process of griefwork which offers real hope that grief will not feel overwhelming forever. You made a difference in their lives and in mine. I have learned and continue to learn from these precious and hurting young ones.

A stream of caring adult professionals and volunteers contributed to the growth and development of this curriculum. The list includes, but is not limited to, Bob Baugher, Ph.D., Dr. Julia E. Fanslow ARNP, Geri Schnitzer-Newson, Nanette Flynn, Shannon Holt, Lissa Smith, Liane Wolbert, the wonderful staff and leadership of Lighthouse Christian Center in Puyallup, WA, and my friend, gifted teacher and encourager, Rae Ann Kelly.

Special thanks go to John Davis for our website design and development, and to Erica Davis for her beautiful, sensitive book cover designs. They have also provided invaluable marketing advice and support.

Brian Montgomery must be the most patient editor that ever was. My heartfelt thanks goes especially to my husband Dave, my family, and to many who are not listed here. I hope you know who you are and how grateful I am to you all.

Kid Talk is a "stand-alone" curriculum; however, it may take place alongside an adult series. It includes an orientation session followed by lesson plans for 13 two-hour sessions for children ages 6 to 12. It contains 103 well-tested activities and games and a wealth of supplemental materials and resources. Customize it to suit your setting, time available, learning styles, and group size. It also works with one child.

The goal of all the Kid Talk activities in the church setting is for each child to get to know God better and trust Him more. In the caring presence of the Kid Talk facilitators, the children have a warm and safe environment to externalize their feelings, process their grief and express their love for their person who died (memorialize).

***Our Story* Memory Book** is 38 pages of exercises crafted to enable children to tell their story and better understand and express their grief. We call it griefwork. It will also help kick-start discussions with family and be a healing reference when children recycle grief in their teen years.

Author's Why

I was a grieving kid. My grandma who lived with us died when I was four years old. My brother was killed when I was twelve. My father died when I was sixteen.

My kids were grieving kids. Their oldest brother died of a brain tumor when they were five and ten. That was in 1983.

Grieving kids are my passion. Caring adults can make a huge difference in their lives, their childhood, and their adolescence. Unresolved childhood grief can contribute to complicated emancipation, adolescent depression, acting out and risk-taking behaviors. It need not be so.

This curriculum and memory book are the result of my many years of working with grieving children. They are roadmaps for anyone willing to be a caring presence and support to young people dealing with death. The activities, play and discussion promote healing through expression of emotions and telling each unique story. They work.

There is no ministry more rewarding than watching hurting children transform back into kids living with zest. May these books give you the confidence and tools you need to give them what they need.

I welcome your feedback. Contact me directly at: mel@kidtalkgrief.com
Or find us on:

Mel Erickson

About the Author

Mel Erickson BA, CT (ret) received her training and experience, working as a social worker and bereavement coordinator for hospice. In 1997 she co-founded a non-profit serving the bereaved community as a resource for education and support.

Mel received National Professional Certification as a Bereavement Facilitator from the American Academy of Bereavement in 1996 and was Certified in Thanatology: Death, Dying and Bereavement by ADEC (Association for Death Education and Counseling) in 2003. Her passion was coming alongside children who had experienced a death. She co-authored *Teen Talk*, an 8-week Curriculum for Grieving Teenagers.

She wrote the *'Our Story' Memory Book* as a tool to help children process their grief. As a presenter, she has spoken and delivered training internationally. She has coordinated the GriefShare ministry at her church and more recently returned to her passion of working with grieving youth.

Mel and her husband have lived in Tacoma, WA since 1976. Three adult children and two adorable grandchildren enrich their lives.

The Objectives of Kid Talk are:

- ➢ to normalize the grieving process,
- ➢ to neutralize fears surrounding the grief experience,
- ➢ to promote healing,
- ➢ to know and trust God as a source of comfort and healing.

These objectives are achieved through repeated storytelling and memorializing activities in a safe and supportive environment. In a support-group setting, it is possible for kids to learn the natural feelings and experiences inherent in the grief process. Their personal processing is normalized by relating their own experiences to the stories of other kids. Understanding grief itself is important to alleviate the fear that comes from a lack of knowledge. Through interactive sharing and play, kids may recognize the similarities of their grief and become more at ease with mourning. In the telling of their story they can allow feelings to surface and give expression to the full emotional gamut surrounding it. We call this "griefwork." It demands our attention, our energy, and our time. It is God-given work we must do in order to "grieve clean" – to heal. The children will learn that doing griefwork is a choice we can make with the realistic hope of healing.

Healing for kids is reflected in their being able to remember and connect with their love for their decedent without the overwhelming pain of sorrow. It is making peace with "goneness" and having energy to invest in living. It does not mean forgetting the person who died or to stop loving them. On the contrary, we find ways to make our love visible – to memorialize – at almost every **Kid Talk** meeting.

While being a caring presence to the children, the **Kid Talk** facilitators model the Language of Grief, thus enabling the therapeutic value of telling and retelling one's story. Kids are given words to go around their feelings and ways to express them. They learn that their grief will recycle as they grow up and by doing griefwork now it can help them later, as will their *Our Story* Memory Books.

Kid Talk facilitators also nurture belief and reliance on God as our trustworthy source of healing, love, strength and hope. The gospel and the Biblical truths about heaven are included in the curriculum. It is our prayer that every child who attends will know God better, and thus trust Him more as they move through their grief journey in **Kid Talk**. We want them, as children of God, to know how to access the presence, comfort and healing power of scripture and their relationship with Christ.

History and Perspective First

Over the last six years, the **Kid Talk Curriculum** and *Our Story* **Memory Book** have been used in a Christian church setting alongside a well-known adult grief curriculum. We have seen broken-hearted and acting-out children, transform before our eyes. What a privilege it is to do this work.

While the activities are appropriate for use in schools, hospice follow-up or private practice, what is laid out here was working in my church until the Covid 19 virus interrupted with the need for social isolation. It is offered as a starting point and is easily modified. As a woman of faith, adding scripture and a biblical perspective makes the curriculum the "full-meal-deal." Our loving God heals and created us to heal through the process of grieving. Children can easily access the grieving process through this curriculum.

Craft your own curriculum. For example, the sessions could be one hour instead of two and there would be enough activities for almost double the number of sessions, depending on whether you include a snack time. Each activity listed in the Curriculum Summary is described in child-friendly language in the Leader's Guide. Each session is accompanied with a Supply List of the required materials. The **Kid Talk** Supply Pantry (pp. 133-137) will tell you where to obtain what you need. The activities are listed alphabetically in the **Kid Talk** Activity Locator on pp. 130-132. The 14-Week Curriculum Overview, "Your Weekly Journey" (a session infographic), and a Lesson Plan Visual are PDFs available at www.kidtalkgrief.com/ktbaccess. They are tools to help you design your own curriculum.

Kid Talk is a grief-support group for bereaved children, ages 6 to 12 and meets for up to two hours, although the sessions are typically around 90 minutes, while the parents or guardians attend their own group. Ideally, this 14-week grief-support program is offered twice a year. Our meeting rooms are next door to each other. The adults assure us they are glad to hear laughter coming from the children – like in our anger session when we pop popcorn, without a lid!

Unless the **Kid Talk** group is small, it might not be possible to complete all the suggested activities in the curriculum. No problem. It is *very* flexible.

Stick with the theme and activities that match the learning styles of your kids in attendance. Remember, not all kids have a "paper and pencil" nature, however, this curriculum contains a variety of activities that should appeal to all learning styles.

The goal of all the **Kid Talk** activities and play, is to provide a warm and welcoming environment where the children are free of judgement. The kids soon learn they are valued and are encouraged to be authentic. They will have the opportunity to externalize the hurtful parts of their grief and express the love they continue to feel for their decedent (memorialize). Kids are comfortable being with other kids who "get it," as they process their grief. One child said, "I didn't know this would be fun!"

In the church context, our goal is to promote the healing of each child's grief, while nurturing their relationship with God. The scripture verses in the curriculum help us to know God and His love for us. As we know God better, it becomes easier to trust Him more with things we do not like and do not understand.

Covid-19 Pandemic

Covid-19 has changed how we are able to work with children at this time in history. ***It is imperative to follow the CDC guidelines for social interaction.*** As of this writing, we are meeting online only and coaching parents or family regarding use of the ***Our Story Memory Book*** and supportive activities, most of which can be done at home with supplies available. We pray the day will soon arrive when we can safely meet face-to-face again with grieving kids in a group setting. Now is the perfect time to plan and prepare for when that day arrives.

For the latest information, please visit our website at www.kidtalkgrief.com.

Kid Talk is a "stand-alone" curriculum and may also take place simultaneously with an adult series. It includes an orientation session followed by lesson plans for 13 two-hour sessions for children ages 6 to 12.

The **Kid Talk** curriculum includes:

1. The *Our Story Memory Book*
2. A one-page lesson plan for each session
3. A Leader's Guide to each session with activity details
4. A Supply List for each session
5. Supplemental materials needed – most are copy machine-ready or printable
6. An Appendix with templates for handouts and tools
    a. A (mostly) theme-based Snack List
    b. A Resource List with Internet links
    c. Sample Registration Forms and Sign-In Sheets

Recommendation - tear apart the Kid Talk Curriculum and separate the material into labeled weekly folders. A hanging file box works well to contain everything you will need for each session. A binder and dividers work fine too.

All suggested supplies, tools and teaching aids are very low cost. Snacks may be the most expensive part of the program, if you have the luxury of time to include them. A lot of the "staples" in your **Kid Talk** Supply Pantry (pp. 133-137,) will last indefinitely or for many group meetings.

Our Story **Memory Book**: our preferred DIY way to package the *Our Story* book for the kids is in a one-inch, 3-ring binder. The photocopied pages are printed then 3-hole punched. The binder allows pages to be removed and/or replaced. Additional pages, i.e. art or worksheets, can be added. Placing a divider or two behind the workbook is a time-saving way to store and access the "Session Logs" and additional completed pages. The plastic cover of a binder serves beautifully as a place to display photos of the decedent and treasured memories.

The *Our Story* **Memory Book** is designed to allow the child to externalize their thoughts and feelings, as well as to document their personal story. It can be interactive with an adult "helper" (facilitator) and with other children in the group. It can serve as a springboard for conversation at home. The children are encouraged to consult someone in their family when they may have trouble completing some of the sections. Every effort is made for the child to value their memory book and keep it in a special place.

It can be an invaluable support to them as they recycle their grief in later years, especially in adolescence, enabling them to reconnect with their once-fresh feelings and perspective of their loss.

Facilitators: a minimum of two adult facilitators and preferably a third, are ideal for **Kid Talk**. Two are required for safety reasons. It is impossible for one facilitator to read all the "cues" in the group, e.g. recognize who might be wanting to share or who may be struggling. A third – perhaps a teen "apprentice" – is a wonderful bonus and can be most helpful with a special-needs or younger child. It is also reassuring to know you have back-up in case of a crisis, so a facilitator can leave the room if necessary. One extra person sure makes clean-up faster.

Room Set-Up: be creative with the space you have. Ideally, three round tables for a small group or three sets of two 6' or 8' tables pushed together when there are 4 or more attending. The facilitators sit with the kids and it is important to be able to see each other's faces when you are sharing. Cover the tables with plastic tablecloths as required by an activity. We use Table 1 for "opening table talk" and *Our Story* book activities. Table 2 is for "focus" and crafts. Table 3 is for snack prep and eating. We return to Table 1 for "closing table talk."

Our room has a TV/DVD player, a white board and a CD player. The WELCOME sign, Sign-In Sheet and handouts for parents are on a table just outside the door. If we have prepared a MEMO for the parents, that is also there. We are very blessed to have such a comfortable space. However, I have gratefully worked with groups in a closet-sized space. We can do what we are called to do, right?

Number of Kids: an ideal number of attendees is 6 to 8 kids, but this depends on your space. A small group can seem really big with just one child who is challenging. Even though we ask for pre-registration, we do get surprise arrivals. We always have more activities than there will be time to finish, so we don't worry about running out of things to do. (The Session Log helps keep track of which activities you have completed or may want to carry over.)

Registration: adults may register on the church website or with the church office staff, if appropriate. Our Registration Form gives us an overview of the ages, kinds of deaths and potential needs of the children who will attend. It is extremely helpful to the facilitators to have completed **Kid Talk** registration packets and the opportunity to interview the parents/guardians before the orientation session. The interview follows the questions asked on the Registration form, found in the Appendix p. 129. This information means we are better prepared for numbers and special needs, and it prompts us to tweak the curriculum to match the anticipated children.

Plus we will also have the correct amounts of craft supplies and snack ingredients. That said, we seldom know exactly who will come, so we guestimate on numbers and intentionally over-prepare. For these reasons, we emphasize with both parents and kids the importance of letting us know in advance if a child will be absent. We are convinced the weekly emails which we send to the parents (and/or children), are pivotal to good attendance. (See below.)

We ask all families to come early to Orientation to complete the following records for each child: (Sample registration forms are on pp. 144 – 147.)

1. **Kid Talk** Registration
2. Image Use Authorization
3. **Kid Talk** Support Group Agreement
4. **Kid Talk** Disclosure/Permission

All who register receive a **Kid Talk** Schedule and sign their child in and out of each meeting.

Plastic Name Card Holders or Tent-Cards: a Dollar Store find and available on Amazon, these have proved to be a valued luxury. The kids make their name place cards the first thing at Orientation. The card stands upright and is visible from both sides so that everyone can see it. This way we quickly learn each other's name. When new kids arrive, it is easy for them to pick up on everyone's name. Before the kids arrive we set out the name place cards strategically in the seating arrangement we think is best. It's a gentle way to assign seats. Tent-cards made from 3"x 5" cards folded in half with the name written on both sides also work well.

Emails: the weekly EMAIL we send to the parents, guardians and/or children is to keep them "in the loop," so they know what their child will be doing in the up-coming session. It helps them to know how to encourage and support their child. We explain the importance of their dialogue and interaction with their child in completing the "take-home griefwork" pages. We want the parents to ask to see and reflect on what their child has brought home and to offer to help them as needed. It is important the parent places value on the "take-home griefwork" and the *Our Story* **Memory Book**. It is good for parents to say, "Where can we keep your **Kid Talk** griefwork so it is easy to find next week? Do you think you can remember it yourself?" The kids generally arrive eager to get to what they know is on the agenda. An email Template and Sample are available on p.140.

Each session of **Kid Talk** is divided into Open, Focus, Snack and Close activities. The general idea is to begin with cognitive activities, work into more emotive activities, and then return to cognitive functioning, so that the children can leave the session in a less fragile state.

"Check-In" is an important part of the Open portion of each session. The children can share about themselves and their lives. They recognize that the facilitators are extremely interested in them and their stories. They begin to establish commonality. We use an assortment of playful ways to help make it easy to share. Wilma the Pop-Up Puppet, dice and the Pop-Up Pirate are favorites.

Photos: using our cell phones, we take photos of the children doing the various activities each week. A group photo, mounted in a frame or on a special page the kids can autograph, is well received. The kids feel remarkably close at the end of 14 weeks. At our last session we show a PowerPoint presentation of our **Kid Talk** time together. We give it to each child on a CD, to put in the pocket of their **Kid Talk** binder. We all enjoy this photo review more than words can express.

Kid Talk Supply Pantry, (pp. 133 – 137 in the Appendix):

Set-up for each **Kid Talk** session takes minimal time if your cupboard is stocked. Of course, you will accumulate tools and materials as you go along. Having learned from experience, we print up all the Session Logs and scripture stickers in one session at the copy machine then file them in the appropriate week's folder. Other items nice to have printed in advance include "Grief Tips Cards," *Someday Heaven* questions, feelings cards, "Tears" poem, "We Will Light Candles" poem, the "stars" poem and Hug Coupons. Printing the weekly Handouts for Adults in advance is also helpful.

How to Use This Curriculum – In a Nutshell

1. You will find Avery printable templates at your exclusive resource page on the website: www.kidtalkgrief.com/ktbaccess. A helpful 14-Week Curriculum Overview, an Infographic of "Your Weekly Journey," and a Lesson Plan Visual Guide are also found there.

2. Start by tearing the curriculum apart as suggested on p. 15. The ***Our Story* Memory Book** is a book in itself. Photocopy it or purchase additional copies on Amazon.

   Please remember the material is copyrighted and for <u>your personal use with grieving children only.</u>

3. If you will be working with more than one or two children at a time, pray and search for the right partner to facilitate with you. For the children's sake and yours, it is important to be a facilitator duo.

4. Be confident you will be able to design a dynamic curriculum to suit your children and setting. You can choose from a large variety of go-to activities well-suited to every learning style and environment.

5. Read the Leader's Guide for details of each activity. Underline or highlight the activities you would like to implement on the **Kid Talk** Lesson Plan page.

6. Stock your **Kid Talk** Pantry as suggested to suit the activities you plan to do.

7. For groups, it is a good idea to arrive an hour early to set up the tables using the Supply List for that week.

8. We pray before each session for each child and family who will attend. We ask for wisdom and welcome the sweet presence of the Holy Spirit. Then we are ready and eager to greet the children.

Kid Talk Lesson Plan – Orientation Week

ORIENTATION: Get Acquainted   **See Leader's Guide for Details**

Scripture & Theme	Activities (minutes) OS = Our Story Memory Book LG = Leaders Guide	Handouts and Take-Home Griefwork

<u>Psalm 147:3</u>
He heals the broken hearted and binds up their wounds.
 	
Sign it with ASL. See www.kidtalkgrief.com /ktbaccess
 	
Pray:
Lord, thank You that You see our broken hearts, You know how much we hurt, and You heal us.
 	
Theme:
Let's Get Acquainted! My Broken Heart
	OPEN: (Approximately **30** minutes)
	Welcome: Flash Paper and Ground Rules with poster
	Learn ASL for Psalm 147:3: discuss and pray.
	Introduce Session Log: discuss and pray.
	Fiddle Things: Stone Hearts or Mosaic Hearts to color.
	Introductions: Name, grade, who died (Use Wilma, the Pop-Up Puppet.)
	(10) Activity: "MOVE!"
	
	FOCUS: (Approximately **55** minutes)
	(10) <u>Acrostic</u> on 9" x 12" envelope using child's name.
	(15) <u>Introduce OS Memory Book:</u> fill in the *OS* title page, discuss pp. 3, 4, and 5:
	Color duck and talk about "What is grief? Bereaved?" "How are you? Just ducky!" "Grief is Like an Onion" and "Tears." Tissues are self-serve. See **LG.**
	(10) <u>My Silent Hurting Heart:</u> *OS* p. 7. Read poem while children are gluing their broken hearts back together. See **LG.**
	(20) <u>Model Magic:</u> Children create something that reminds them of the person who died. Allow to dry on wax paper until next week.
	   • **Read *EMILY LOST SOMEONE SHE LOVED*** by Kathleen Fucci while the children are working.
	   • **Take Smile on A Stick photos.**
	
	SNACK: (Approximately **20** minutes) –
	Cheese (cookie cutter hearts) and Ritz crackers
	
	CLOSE: (Approximately **15** minutes)
	Someday Heaven: read and discuss one question.
	<u>Session Log</u>
	<u>Take-Home Griefwork</u>
	<u>Prayer</u>
		Handouts for Adults:
		"**Kid Talk** Grief Support Objectives" - (**Kid Talk** Curriculum p. 12)
		
		Handouts for Kids:
		• *Our Story* **Memory Books** in 1" binders with a section divider for the Session Logs
		• Session Log and Bible Verse Stickers
		• 9" x 12" envelope
		• 2 red, paper hearts for each child (for *OS* p. 7)
		
		Take-Home Griefwork:
		• *OS* p. 8
		  "All About Me"
		• Bring photo/s for cover of binder.
		
		Next Week:
		• Introduce decedents with photos.
		• Receive Smile on a Stick photos.
		• Share "All About Me."
		• Paint Model Magic sculptures.
		• Put our tears in a bottle.

NOTES

These activities are used in conjunction with the 14-week Kid Talk Curriculum and the *Our Story* Memory Book for children.

NOTE: The Language of Grief includes lots of new words for the children. There is a Glossary on pp. 148 to 151. You can print the glossary as cards from our website at www.kidtalkgrief.com/ktbaccess. The cards can be used as you introduce a few words each week and for the Glossary Match Game in Week 13.

The following activities are described approximately in the order in which they appear in the curriculum.

ASL Psalm 147:3 – this is the theme scripture for the entire **Kid Talk** series. We open every session by signing this verse in American Sign Language (ASL). There is a demonstration at www.kidtalkgrief.com/ktbaccess. After a couple of weeks, the children will lead this activity. Print the verse on self-adhesive Avery 5395 Name Badges which the kids will apply to their Session Log. A printable version is available at www.kidtalkgrief.com/ktbaccess.

Session Log: each **Kid Talk** session begins and ends with the Session Log. The child records their name and the date. Review the theme for the week by reading it aloud together or having the children take turns reading. In addition to Psalm 147:3, there is a new verse and accompanying prayer each week. The verse is printed out on a label which the child applies to their session log. Read the verse together. Discuss its meaning. Pray the written prayer together.

Return to the Session Log for the closing portion of each **Kid Talk** session. The child circles or underlines the activities they completed and then checks the box for what they liked best. (Some weeks not all the activities get done.) Ask them to explain their choice. They also fill in what they want to remember from this session. The Session Logs are filed behind a divider tab in the *Our Story* binder. They serve as a reminder of what happened at **Kid Talk** as well as a springboard for discussion at home. A second divider tab is useful to designate additional pages completed by the child.

Ground Rules: make a laminated copy of the Ground Rules included in this week's materials (p. 28) to refer to each week. (You can print it in color from: www.kidtalkgrief.com/ktbaccess.) This sheet should be reviewed at the beginning of the first few sessions, then as needed, especially if new children join the group.

The most important rules are summarized by "confidentiality" and "respect." (What we say here, stays here. The exception is that you can talk to your family about what you said and did at **Kid Talk**.) Soon the children will tell you the ground rules without needing the graphic.

Explain that tissues are self-serve because if we hand you a tissue, you might think that you shouldn't cry. Tears are OK!

Wilma: is a Pop-Up Puppet named by the children because she looks like Mrs. Fred Flintstone. She is easily made and worth her weight in gold.

Talking through Wilma gives most children a voice when otherwise they might not find the words. Wilma is always available to do the talking. She is small and portable. The children will make Wilma puppets at our last session together. DIY instructions are included with Week 13, (p. 125). You can purchase a ready-made kit to make 12 puppets. See p. 136.

Fiddle Things: we keep a collection of "fiddle things" in a labeled tub. (Examples include heart shaped stones, Apache tears, shells, buckeyes, pecans, colored glass discs etc.) Studies show that engaging small muscles with motor activity increases the ability to listen and internalize what is heard. They may also be used to open a session. Pass the basket of fiddle things. Each child takes a turn choosing a fiddle thing, sharing "check-in" and then passes the basket to the next person. Similarly, the process can be repeated at the close of the session by returning the fiddle things to the basket while sharing something specific. With some groups, the fiddle things may become a distraction. Coloring the worksheets or mandalas achieves the same result.

Mandalas and Mazes: see Coloring Pages in the **Kid Talk** Supply Pantry for URLs. We keep a binder of coloring pages for easy retrieval. (Appendix pp. 133 - 137.)

Mosaic Heart Coloring Page: this page is found at www.supercoloring.com/coloring-pages/heart-mosaic. (Appendix pp. 133 - 137.)

Move!: this is a powerful ice breaker exercise. The script is included with the Orientation Session Lesson Plan (p. 29). The leader reads the "descriptor phrase" and then directs the children where to go in the room. The first items are simple and not emotionally loaded. As the exercise continues, the descriptors become more personal and death related. This activity allows the children to see and experience how much they have in common. It quickly establishes they are with other kids who "get it."

Flash Paper: Flash Paper is a flammable tissue that may be purchased from a magic supply resource online or at a magic shop. (Appendix p. 129.) The leader says, "We are here together because someone important to us has died. We all understand when someone dies your whole life can change in a flash – just like this!" Then the leader holds up the flash paper and touches it with a flame. It flashes! Kids often want to see it again. If so, invite one of them to hold the paper and another to say the words. It's probably best for the leader to light the match. (Make sure that the child holding the flash paper does not have damp fingers which might cause the flash paper to stick.)

Acrostics: each child receives a 9" x 12" envelope to transport both completed work and their "take-home griefwork," if desired. Creating an acrostic on the envelope validates the importance and uniqueness of each child. Instruct the children to write their name vertically. Then they will write a word or phrase that describes who they are and what they like to do. Asking one another for descriptive words that start with a specific letter is an icebreaker and helps with getting acquainted. It is fun to help one another discover descriptive words that match how a person sees him or herself.

Just Ducky: found on p. 3 of **OS**, this illustration can be colored while discussing its content and meaning. It is useful for learning the definitions of "bereaved" and "grief." It validates how we look on the outside to other people but it may not be how we are feeling on the inside. Sometimes, when people ask how we are doing, the answer is not "fine." So, to each other we can say, "Just ducky, thank you!" meaning while we may look composed and unruffled on the outside, on the inside, we are paddling like crazy. This is a "code" the children can share with their family. They may even want an extra copy to take home and put on the refrigerator. **FYI: Bereaved** people are grieving the death of a person. Bereavement is a specific kind of grief because we grieve many kinds of losses. Carl Jung, the eminent Swiss psychologist and psychiatrist, said every change is a loss and every loss must be grieved. Grieving many changes or losses at once, including a death, is compound grief and deserves special treatment and support.

Silent Hurting Heart: to save time, precut two red hearts for each child. (Pattern provided on p. 30.) Invite the children to "take one heart and tear it apart to show you how your heart has been torn apart because someone important to you has died." (Be prepared for confetti.) Then ask them to scribble on the back of the second heart and then tear it apart, knowing they will be putting it back together like a puzzle. They will apply glue to the back side and glue their healing heart to p. 7 of their **Our Story** Memory **Book**. As they are working, comment "how much work it is to put a broken heart back together and it can take a long time." Read and discuss the narrative at the bottom of the page.

Model Magic: Model Magic is a clay-like product by Crayola. Use white so the children can color their sculptures with markers. We purchase it with discount coupons at a local craft store. Invite the children to create something that reminds them of their decedent i.e. person who died. Or they may choose to make a pendant with a hole at the top that can become a necklace. Their creations are stored on a tray or cookie sheet covered with wax paper to dry until the next session. The sculptures are very lightweight and fragile but color very nicely with markers. At the next session, be prepared to wrap their creations for travel. We use tissue and food take-out boxes.

Photo with Smile-on-A-Stick: the child selects a smile on a stick in their preferred skin tone. (See the **Kid Talk** Supply Pantry in the Appendix on pp. 133 - 137.) This is a companion activity with the duck illustration. Take a photo of each child with sad eyes behind the smile-on-a-stick to have printed and distributed at the next session. They may choose to put their photo inside the plastic cover of their *Our Story* binder. It is both unifying and validating to see that your friends are experiencing the same sad and difficult realities as you while putting on a "happy face." Take the photos while the kids are sculpting their Model Magic.

'Emily Lost Someone She Loved': by Kathleen Fucci. Read this story to the children while they are working on their Model Magic projects.

Snacks*: **Kid Talk** snacks are object lessons designed to be interactive and symbolically connected to the theme of the session as much as possible. For example, heart shaped cookies that can be decorated, broken, and eaten would be a good review of "Our Silent Hurting Hearts." Another (simpler) option for the Orientation week is to cut cheese slices with heart shaped cookie cutters sized to fit on a Ritz cracker. A list of snack options is supplied in the Appendix on p. 138. You may want a snack that reflects a holiday season.

*Please follow CDC recommendations for food safety at
www.cdc.gov/foodsafety/newsletter/food-safety-and-Coronavirus.html

'Someday Heaven': by Larry Libby. This book answers questions about heaven likely to be on the mind of a child. We have printed, laminated, and cut apart the 14 questions about heaven addressed in the book. We keep them in a "butterfly box" from the Dollar Store. Each week a different child draws a question topic to be read from the book. He or she then either reads the appropriate page or chooses someone else to read it.

After being read, the question card is tucked into an envelope kept in the box. The *'Someday Heaven'* questions template is included with this lesson. To print a larger version, visit www.kidtalkgrief.com/ktbaccess.

Take Home Griefwork: the 9"x 12" envelopes are for transporting "take-home griefwork." (We **do not** refer to it as homework.) Some children prefer to take their *Our Story* **Memory Books** home to work on them. A small amount of "take-home griefwork" is assigned at the end of each session because, 1. The children don't always know the answers to the questions that need to be filled in, and 2. It generates dialogue between the child and their parents, guardian and/or siblings. They are then doing griefwork with someone else who cares about the person who died. We emphasize the value of the completed *Our Story* **Memory Book**. Its value increases with the number of completed pages it has. We explain to the children they will grieve again as they grow up, especially in their teen years. Their *Our Story* **Memory Book** will help them remember and process their grief when that time comes.

The Weekly EMAIL: please refer to p. 17 where we explain the significance of these regular communications we send to the parents or guardians.

Note: we print out extra *Our Story* pages to have available at the group session. We may give stickers or tickets (See Tickets on p. 36) as a reward to those who return with their books. Every group is a little different and may be motivated differently. Some kids are not 'paper-and-pencil' oriented. Fortunately, there are plenty of interactive activities for them to be fully engaged most of the time.

Find Your Way

Kid Talk Supply List – Orientation Week

- Handouts for Parents/Guardians: "**Kid Talk** Grief Support Objectives"
- Handouts for the Kids: Session Log and Bible Verse Stickers, 2 red paper hearts for each child, Mosaic Heart coloring page
- Clipboard with Sign-In Sheet, pen and WELCOME sign
- Name Place Cards or Tent name cards and 3"x 5" for new attendees
- 1" binder for each child containing the **Our Story** Memory Book and a divider labeled "Session Logs"
- Ground Rules poster
- Wilma, Pop-Up-Puppet
- Book: '*Someday Heaven*' by Larry Libby
- Glossary Cards from www.kidtalkgrief.com/ktbaccess
- Hand Sanitizer

- Plastic tablecloths for Tables 2 and 3
- Pencils
- Pens
- Markers
- Box of tissues
- Basket of fiddle things (heart shaped stones etc.)
- Flash paper and matches or a lighter
- Script for "MOVE"
- Sample acrostics
- *Someday Heaven* cards in a box

- Smile-on-a Stick(s) and camera to take photos
- 9" x 12" envelopes
- Model Magic and scissors to open the bag it comes in
- Tray or cookie sheet and wax paper for drying sculptures
- Snack: Different colors of cheese slices, Ritz crackers and an assortment of small heart-shaped cookie cutters
- Paper plates, plastic knives and napkins
- Pitcher of water and cups

Room Set Up:

Be creative with the space that you have. We use three tables; round or two 6' tables pushed together. It is important to be able to see each other's faces when you are sharing. We cover the tables with plastic tablecloths as required by an activity.

Kid Talk Session Log – Orientation Week

Date: _____

Theme: Let's Get Acquainted. My Broken Heart.

Series Scripture: *He heals the broken-hearted and binds up their wounds. Psalm 147:3.*

Scripture: Put scripture sticker here ➡
Psalm 147:3

Pray:
Lord, thank You that You see our broken hearts, You know how much we hurt, and You heal us.

My <u>favorite</u> activity about this session:

☐ Learning ASL   ☐ Meeting Other   ☐ 'MOVE!'   ☐ Acrostic About Me
for Psalm 147:3   Grieving Kids

☐ *My Silent*   ☐ Model Magic   ☐ *Emily Lost*   ☐ Snack – Cheese
Hurting Heart   *Someone She*   Hearts and Ritz Crackers
                                              Loved

Explain your choice: _____

_____

What I want to remember from this session: _____

_____

_____

Signature _____

Respect One Another

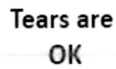
Tears are OK

Be responsible for your own learning

You have the option to pass

Confidentiality ! ! !

Expect unfinished business

Start and stop on time

Speak for yourself

MOVE!

This is an icebreaker that reveals commonalities. It is similar to musical chairs. Place chairs in a circle equal to the number of people. The leader reads a statement and if the answer is yes, then the participants must move to an empty chair. About 20 statements are read, beginning with very general statements and getting more personal. Facilitators also participate. Alternately, participants can be sent to different places in the room If a statement applies to them. (Example: "If you love ice cream, go to that corner!")

- Everyone who is wearing blue jeans, **MOVE!**
- If you love pizza, **MOVE!**
- If you like burgers and fries better than pizza, **MOVE**!
- If you have a vegetarian in your family, **MOVE!**
- If you've gone to the movies within the last month, **MOVE!**
- If you were born out of this state, **MOVE!**
- If you've lived outside of the United States, **MOVE!**
- If you like to play tennis, ping pong or racquet sports, **MOVE!**
- If you play football or wrestle, **MOVE!**
- If you are a swimmer, a skier or a snow boarder, **MOVE!**
- If you've changed schools within the last year, **MOVE!**
- If you have pierced ears or pierced something else, **MOVE!**
- If you've had a disagreement with your parents about pierced ears, **MOVE!**
- If you have a tattoo or want to get a tattoo, **MOVE!**
- If you've had a pet die, **MOVE!**
- If you've had a funeral for a pet, **MOVE!**
- If you've visited a sick person in the hospital, **MOVE!**
- If you've been to a cemetery, **MOVE!**
- If you listen to music when you're sad, **MOVE!**
- If you've felt like crying while listening to music, **MOVE!**
- If you've had a disagreement with a friend in the last 2 weeks, **MOVE!**
- If you've made peace with that friend after the argument, **MOVE!**
- If you've had a good friend move away, **MOVE!**
- If you've had to move away from your friends, **MOVE!**
- If you've had an argument with your parents within the last 2 weeks, **MOVE!**
- If you've made peace with your parents after the argument, **MOVE!**
- If you think it is harder to talk to your parents now, than it was when you were a little kid, **MOVE!**
- If someone you love has died, **MOVE!**
- If your grandpa or grandma has died, **MOVE!**
- If you've had a brother or sister die, **MOVE!**
- If you think life is unfair, **MOVE!**

Cut Two for each child.

How can I know for sure I am going to heaven?	Will anyone meet me when I get to heaven?	How long does it take to get to heaven?
Will my grandpa still be old in heaven?	Will I be an angel when I get to heaven?	Will I need money in heaven?
Will there be children in heaven?	Will I ever be sad in heaven?	How long will I be in heaven?
Will it always be light in heaven?	How do I get to heaven?	Will my pets go to heaven?
Where is heaven?	Who lives in heaven?	**Question Cards For** *Someday Heaven*

Kid Talk Schedule (Sample)

Location

Session	Date	Theme	Scripture
	Sept. 5th	My Broken Heart	Psalm 147:3**
1	Sept. 12th	My Grief Is Unique	Psalm 61:2B
2	Sept 19th	Meet My Person Who Died	Isaiah 61:1b-2
3	Sept 26th	The Funeral or Memorial	Psalm 46:1
4	Oct. 3rd	My "Grief Bundle"	Psalm 130:5
5	Oct. 10th	Feelings of Grief	Psalm 34:18
6	Oct. 17th	Anger and Guilt	Deuteronomy 29:29a
7	Oct. 24th	Griefwork: What Is It?	Psalm 139:16b
	Oct. 31st	**NO MEETING**	
8	Nov. 7th	Imprints – Their Mark on My Life	Isaiah 26:3 NLT
	Nov. 10h	**Surviving the Holidays Workshop**	
9	Nov. 14st	Dreams and Trust	Proverbs 3:5 NLT
	Nov. 21st	**NO MEETING**	
10	Nov. 28th	Memories	Philippians 4:13 NLT
11	Dec. 5th	Gratitude	Romans 5:8
12	Dec. 12th	Heaven	Revelation 21:4
13	Dec. 19th	Hope & How to Help Others	Isaiah 40:51
14	Dec. 26th	Celebrate!	Psalm 147:3

All sessions are from 6:30 to 8:30 p.m. in Room 10. *Note: There is no meeting 10/31 or 11/21.*

** Psalm 147:3 is our theme scripture. We open each meeting by signing it in addition to the scripture verse of the week.

"Take Home Griefwork" is an important part of Kid Talk. Each child receives an *Our Story Memory Book* that will help him or her tell his or her story, understand the grieving process better, and process their grief with other kids who 'get it,' and with their families. The child may choose to take pages home in a big envelope to complete or take the whole book back and forth to Kid Talk.

Keep the *Our Story Memory Book* in a safe place so you know where it is when it is time to travel!

Leadership Team: (Please call or email us with questions or to let us know that you will miss a session. It helps us plan and we pray for you!)

Name
Contact Information

Name
Contact Information

Name
Contact information

Name
Contact Information

Kid Talk Lesson Plan – Week 1

Week 1: I am Unique
See Leader's Guide for Details

Scripture & Theme	Activities (minutes) OS = *Our Story* Memory Book LG = Leader's Guide	Handouts and Take-Home Griefwork
Psalm 61:1b-2 NLT *I cry to You for help when my heart is overwhelmed. Lead me to the towering rock of safety.* **Pray:** Dear Lord, help us to remember to cry out to You when our hearts are overwhelmed; when we hurt so much that we don't have words. Lead us to a place where we can feel safe and be comforted. Thank You for **Kid Talk**. **Theme:** I am unique and my grief is unique too.	**OPEN:** (Approximately **30** minutes) As children arrive, work on coloring Model Magic sculptures or *OS* p. 8. **Welcome:** Ground Rules with poster **Psalm 147: 3:** ASL, discuss & pray. **Session Log:** Psalm 61:1b-2 NLT, discuss and pray. **Check-In:** Roll a single die for introductions: # on die = how many things are shared from the "All About Me" on *OS* p. 8. **Distribute "Smile-on-A-Stick" photos.** Kids may choose to place their photos inside the cover of their binder. **Share Decedent photos and *OS* p. 9**. Place them in binder cover. Look at *OS* p. 11 and begin acrostics for the decedents. **FOCUS:** (Approximately **55** minutes) **(10) "Where do you stand?"** Create a scale with 15' – 20' of masking tape on the floor. Write a "1" on the left end and a "10" on the right end. Using the "Where I Stand" script, ask kids to stand on the tape "where you stand" on the topic. (1=none or hardly at all and 10 = a lot or very much.) See **LG**. **(10) Craft Stick Exercise.** See **LG**. **(10) Uniquely Me:** Refer to Leader's Guide and print puzzle. **(15) *Tear Soup*:** watch the video or read the book. **(10) Tears in a Bottle:** OS p. 5. Practice saying the "Tears" poem together. See **LG**. **SNACK:** (Approximately **20** minutes) Dulce de Leche and Apple Wedges **CLOSE:** (Approximately **15** minutes) ***Someday Heaven*: Read and discuss one question.** **Session Log** **Take-Home Griefwork** **Happy Snaps:** Refer to **LG** **Prayer**	**Handouts for Adults:** *"Helping Your Child Through Grief"* by Alan D. Wolfelt, Ph.D. **Handouts for Kids:** • Session Log • Bible Verse Stickers • Uniquely Me • Mandalas or heart coloring sheets **Take-Home Griefwork:** • *OS*: p. 9 "Meet My___" • *OS*: p. 11 "Acrostic" **Next week:** • Talk more about the decedent. • Share "Favorite Things" and "Acrostics." • Begin to explore the feelings of grief. • Paint rocks.

NOTES

Note: Activities previously described will not be repeated. Refer to the **Kid Talk** Activity Locator in the Appendix (pp. 130 – 132).

Scripture Verse: this week's verse is Psalm 61:2b NLT. Print on Avery Name Badges 5395.

Check-In with Dice Roll Introductions: a dry erase block on which you've written the numbers works as well as a traditional die. Each child rolls the die, counts the dots or calls out the number and then shares that many things about him or herself referring to "All About Me" on p. 8 of *Our Story*.

Craft Stick Exercise: invite each child to draw themselves on the stick. Say, "Last week we tore hearts apart to illustrate our broken hearts. Now, break your stick into two pieces. Hold them up in front of you. Are any of them broken the same? No! Remember Tear Soup? We all grieve differently, and our 'brokenness' looks different. We are as unique in our grief as we are in our personalities and how we look. This means when someone says, 'I understand how you feel,' it is not likely they really do. It is better to say, 'I remember what it was like for me. What is it like for you?'"

Uniquely Me: invite the children to fill in the puzzle pieces as indicated. Each child may roll the die to come up with a number, then chooses someone else in the group to "interview" by asking that many questions from the "Uniquely Me" page. Discuss how different and yet the same we are. Our grief is as different as we are. There is no right or wrong way to grieve but it is important to choose to <u>do</u> "griefwork" in order to heal. We're doing griefwork at **Kid Talk**. (This may be a good time to review what "griefwork" is. See *Our Story* p. 26.) Share Zephaniah 3:17 NIV "The Lord your God is with you; He is mighty to save. He will take great delight in you, He will quiet you with His love, He will rejoice over you with singing."

Tear Soup: *"Tear Soup, A Recipe for Healing After Loss"* is a book and a video. We have found the children to be more attentive to the video. The book can be read to them while they are eating their snack if time is running short.

Where do you stand?: Create a scale with masking tape on the floor and read the statements listed on p. 38. This activity enables children to see and experience what they have in common. It validates their uniqueness while at the same time it generates bonding.

Tears in a Bottle: provide 1 or 2-ounce bottles with a secure cork or lid, a couple of measuring cups with pour spouts, water and food colors. Make labels for the bottles, if desired (Avery template available at www.kidtalkgrief.com/ktbaccess.) The bottles can be decorated with ribbon, flowers, stickers, etc. The children can collectively decide what color to make their tears. Psalm 56:8 says, "You have taken note of my journey through life, caught each of my tears in Your bottle." This verse is available as a PDF for adhesive labels at www.kidtalkgrief.com/ktbaccess. They are indelible memories. These little bottles of tears remind us of this important truth. Recite together the "Tears" poem on p. 5 of *Our Story*.

Happy Snaps: are when you close your eyes and picture the person who died doing something that makes you smile. It is an indelible memory. Sharing "happy snaps" at the end of a session (for kids and adults) helps bring us back to cognitive function and a happy place. A "happy snap" is an indelible memory snapshot.

Snack: Dulce de Leche, is Spanish for "sweet of milk." It is made by gently boiling a can of condensed milk under water for two hours. <u>Cool thoroughly</u> before opening the can. The result is a caramel-like dip for (green) apple wedges or pears. Store refrigerated in a covered container. Invite the children to spoon out some Dulce de Leche onto their plates for dipping. Use an apple corer/wedge cutter to cut the apples. Place the apple on a cutting board on the seat of a chair, making it low enough for the kids to apply the pressure needed to cut through the apple. Allow one apple per child.

OPTIONAL ACTIVITIES:

Keep the supplies for these activities handy to use as needed or when they might be appropriate.

Beaded Bracelets: bracelet elastic and lots of alphabet beads and spacer "pony" beads are all that are needed for this project. The children like to make the name of their loved one who died. They help each other find specific letters. This is a good "icebreaker" or "filler" activity to have on hand. If the attendance is low, it is easy to run through all the planned activities. The bracelet is a popular way to "memorialize."

Tickets: tickets can serve as positive reinforcement for children participating well and staying on task. Use them as rewards for contributing to the discussion, being a good listener, remembering well, etc. Save the tickets for a future drawing. We seldom use them as they are just not needed. However, some temperaments respond very well to this kind of motivation. The tickets are good to have as a "back-up" plan.

- Handouts for Parents/Guardians: "Helping Your Child Through Grief" by Alan D. Wolfelt Ph.D.
- Handouts for Kids: Session Log and Bible Verse Stickers, Uniquely Me, Mandalas or heart coloring sheets
- Clipboard with Sign-In Sheet, pen and WELCOME sign
- Supplies to make name cards for new arrivals
- *Our Story* binder
- Ground Rules poster
- Wilma, Pop-Up-Puppet
- Book: '*Someday Heaven*' by Larry Libby
- Glossary Cards from www.kidtalkgrief.com/ktbaccess
- Hand Sanitizer

• Basket of fiddle things (Apache Tears)	• Mosaic hearts, mandalas or coloring sheets
• A single die (dice)	• Smile-on-A-Stick(s) and camera to take photos
• Masking tape/permanent marker	• 9" x 12" envelopes (for new arrivals)
• Script for "Where do you stand?"	• Dried Model Magic sculptures and colored markers
• *Tear Soup* book by Pat Schwiebert and Chuck DeKlyen *Tear Soup video is an attention-holding option.*	• Tissue paper and Chinese boxes or alternative packaging for taking home fragile Model Magic sculptures
• Tears in a Bottle: 1 or 2 oz. bottles with secure lids, pitcher of water, measuring cups, whisk, food coloring, plastic dinner plates, 1 qt. zip lock baggies. Optional: hot glue gun to seal the jar lids and Psalm 56:8 labels.	• Bead bracelets and supplies to make name bracelets (optional)
• Large craft sticks, markers and extra fine permanent markers for drawing faces.	• Tickets for reward drawing (optional)
	• Snack: Dulce de Leche

Room Set up: three tables for opening, focus and snack. A tablecloth makes the snack table easy to distinguish.

Kid Talk Session Log - Week 1

Date: _____

Theme: I am unique. My grief is also unique.

Series Scripture: *He heals the broken-hearted and binds up their wounds. Psalm 147:3.*

Scripture: Put scripture sticker here ➡
Psalm: 61:2b NLT

Pray:
Dear Lord, help us to remember to cry out to You when our hearts are over-whelmed; when we hurt so much that we do not have words. Lead us to a place where we can feel safe and be comforted. Thank You for Kid Talk.

My <u>favorite</u> activity about this session:

☐ Scriptures   ☐ Where Do I Stand?   ☐ Tears in a Bottle   ☐ Craft Stick Exercise

☐ Uniquely Me   ☐ Tear Soup   ☐ *Someday Heaven*   ☐ Snack- Dulce de Leche

Explain your choice: _____

_____

What I want to remember from this session: _____

_____

_____

Signature _____

Where Do I Stand? - Activity

Use masking tape to create a line on the floor. This line represents a scale of how strongly you feel or experience what is mentioned. If you feel strongly, stand on the line near the 10. If you do not have that feeling or experience, stand at the 1. You may want to stand somewhere in between.
We'll start with two easy samples:

- You love chocolate.
- You love cooked spinach.

OK! YOU HAVE SUFFERED A LOSS AND MAY EXPERIENCE ANY OF THE FOLLOWING RESPONSES TO SOME DEGREE.
(All are *normal* examples of kids' grief responses after someone has died.)

- You feel tightness in your throat or heaviness in your chest.
- You have an empty feeling in your stomach and lose your appetite.
- You feel guilty at times, and angry at others.
- You feel restless and look for activity but find it difficult to concentrate.
- You feel as though the loss isn't real, that it didn't happen.
- You sense your loved one's presence, like expecting him or her to walk in the door at the usual time, hearing his or her voice, or seeing his or her face.
- You wander aimlessly and forget or don't finish things you've started at home or at school.
- You have difficulty sleeping, and dream of your loved one.
- You assume mannerisms and traits of your loved one.
- You feel guilty or angry over things that happened in your relationship with the decedent.
- You feel angry at the loved one for leaving you.
- You feel as though you need to take care of the other people.
- You politely don't talk about your feelings or loss.
- You need to tell and retell and remember things about your loved one.
- It helps you to talk about the experience of your decedent's death.
- Your mood changes over the slightest thing.
- You are surprised or feel attacked by waves of grief.
- You have feelings of emptiness or sadness.
- You cry at unexpected things.
- You have felt that the death was your fault.
- You feel "not normal" since your person died.
- You feel like you might be grieving all by yourself.
- You think you do not know everything that you need to know about the death.
- You isolate or seal yourself off from others more than you used to.
- You lack energy to even do fun stuff.
- You have been more afraid of the dark since the death. Of being away from your parents?
- You have had more conflict with your parents since the death.
- Your schoolwork has suffered, or your grades gone down.

THESE ARE ALL NATURAL AND NORMAL GRIEF RESPONSES.

My favorite place to go when I want to be alone

If I won a million dollars, I would...

Uniquely Me

A piece of clothing that my parents don't like me to wear...

My best time of the day is...

because...

When I am old, I still want to be able to...

Something that is hard for me to do is...

Something that is easy for me to do is...

Kid Talk Lesson Plan – Week 2

Week 2: The Person Who Died

See Leader's Guide for Details

Scripture & Theme	Activities (minutes) OS = *Our Story* Memory Book LG = Leader's Guide	Handouts and Take-Home Griefwork
Isaiah 61:1b-2 *He has sent me [Jesus]....to comfort all who mourn.* **Pray:** Lord Jesus, thank You for sending the Holy Spirit to comfort us. Thank You for giving us **Kid Talk**. Please comfort each child here today/ tonight. **Theme:** Introduce the person who died, (decedent.)	**OPEN**: (Approximately **30** minutes) **Welcome:** Ground Rules with poster Psalm 147:3 ASL, discuss & pray. **Session Log**: Isaiah 61:1b-2, discuss & pray. **Check-In** with Toilet Paper: share from *OS* pp. 8, 9 or 10. Let Wilma do the introductions or be the interviewer. See **LG** **FOCUS**: (Approximately **55** minutes) **(15) Meet My**: *OS* p. 9 (or child may choose *OS* p. 10) **Favorite Things**: *OS* p. 10. Ask each child to share the favorite things of the person who died. **(10) An Acrostic for :** *OS* p. 12. Each child will share their acrostic about their decedent. Suggest they copy their acrostic onto their big manila envelope. See **LG**. **(10) Alphabet Poem**: *OS* p. 13. As time allows, ask the children to remember their decedents. Explain this is their take-home griefwork. It's great to get their family's input on the Alphabet Poem. **(20) Paint Rocks:** invite the children to paint up to 3 rocks that tell something about their decedent or their feelings. **SNACK**: (Approximately **20** minutes) Ants on a Log or Seasonal Choice **CLOSE**: (Approximately **15** minutes) *Someday Heaven:* Read and discuss one question. **Complete Session Log** **Review Take-Home Griefwork** **Happy Snaps** **Prayer**	**Handouts for Adults:** *"Is My Child's Grief Normal?"* By Mel Erickson **OR** a copy of *"12 Simple Tips & Tools To Help Your Grieving Child"* by Mel Erickson **Handouts for Kids:** • *Our Story* binders • Session Log • Bible Verse Stickers • Mandalas, mazes, or coloring pages **Take-Home Griefwork:** • Alphabet Poem *(OS* pp. 13 & 14) • My Experience with Death *(OS* p. 15) **Next Week:** • We'll use the flannel board to tell about the funeral or memorial service. • Make votive candles. • Create our own ritual to remember our decedents.

NOTES

Reminder: Activities previously described will not be repeated. Please refer to previous lessons or the Activity Locator on pp. 130 - 132.

Toilet Paper Check-In: using a roll of toilet paper with squares, each child tears off "as much toilet paper as you think you will need" from the roll. When everyone has a length of toilet paper, ask them to count their squares. Then say, "OK! Who has the most squares? You'll start. Tell us that many things about yourself." They can use their "All About Me" or "Uniquely Me" pages to select what they want to share about themselves, preferably **something new** the group does not already know. Sometimes it is fun to ask the other group members to share things they know about the person whose turn it is. OR they may choose to share things about their decedent, referring to **Our Story** pp. 8, 9 and 10.

Meet My_: *OS* p. 9. Ask the children to fill in the blanks. They will write the title (i.e. mom, dad, sister, etc.) and name of the person who died. Writing the name allows them to express love for their decedent. They can write down things they remember about the person or just draw a picture. (One little boy drew a picture of his dad working as a telephone line repair man.) This is a good time to share photos of the decedents.

Favorite Things: *OS* p. 10. This is a great page for remembering the person who died, as a family. If a child doesn't have all the answers, suggest he ask someone. Who might know?. There is tremendous value in remembering together as a family. There may even be disagreement about "grandpa's favorite food." There may be laughter at uniqueness or because someone else in the family likes the same things. There may be stories connected to the favorite things that need to be told.

An Acrostic for____: the acrostic makes it possible to describe the person who died with just a few words using the letters of their name. The acrostic can be recorded on p. 12 of **Our Story** or on the 9"x12" manila envelope. (An acrostic for the child was done at the first session.) Invite the children to help each other think up words that fit. If you are able, offer to prepare a "fancy" computer graphic of their acrostic suitable for framing or to keep in their **Our Story** binder.

Alphabet Poem: this a challenging but fun way to describe the person who died. Use the sample on *OS* p. 13 for inspiration and fill in the blanks on p. 14. Send this page home with the children to finish with the help of their family. Working on it together as griefwork can stimulate memories and conversation among family members. This is a good thing. It means the child is not doing griefwork alone, but with others who also love the person who died.

Paint Rocks: supplies needed include tempera paints, small brushes, a small paint palette and paper cup of water for each pair of children, and 2 or 3 clean smooth rocks for each child. Spray the painted rocks with acrylic spray when dry. They may not be ready to take home until next week.

Snack: Ants on a Log. Wash and cut celery sticks to about 4" lengths. Each child gets a napkin, small paper plate and a plastic knife. They may fill their celery with cream cheese or peanut butter and put raisins (black ants) or craisins (red ants) on the "log." Ants come uninvited. So does grief. Ants get everywhere and are intrusive. So is grief; it impacts every aspect of our lives. Ants are hard to get rid of and they come back. So does grief. Ask the children to think of other ways ants and grief might be alike.

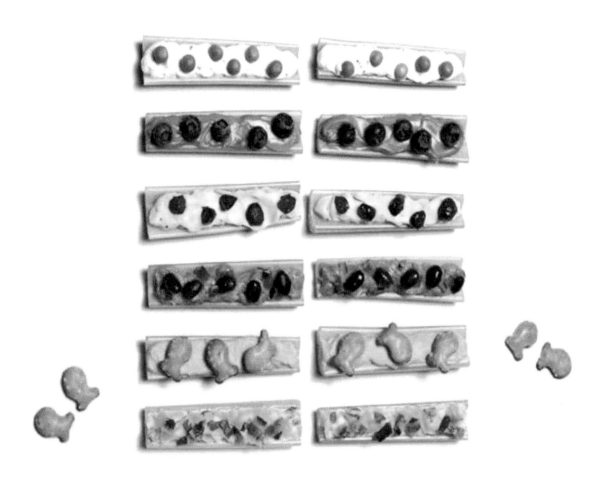

Ants on a Log By FoodNetwork

- Handouts for Parents/Guardians: "Is My Child's Grief Normal?"
- Handouts for Kids: Session Log and Bible Verse Stickers, Mandalas, mazes or coloring pages
- Clipboard with Sign-In Sheet, pen and WELCOME sign
- Supplies to make name place cards for new arrivals
- *Our Story* binder
- Ground Rules poster
- Wilma, Pop-Up-Puppet
- Book: *'Someday Heaven'* by Larry Libby
- Glossary Cards from www.kidtalkgrief.com/ktbaccess
- Hand Sanitizer

- Plastic table cloth for Tables 2 and 3	- Mandalas and coloring sheets
- Pencils	- Bead bracelet supplies (optional)
- Pens	- Tickets (optional)
- Markers	- Snack: Ants on a Log
- Box of tissues	- Paper plates, plastic knives and napkins
- Basket of fiddle things (optional)	- Pitcher of water and small cups
- Roll of sectioned toilet paper	
- Smooth rocks, tempera paints, paint palettes, brushes, newspaper for drying tray and acrylic spray	

Room Set Up:

We cover both the craft and snack tables with a plastic cloth for this session.

Kid Talk Session Log - Week 2

Date: _____

Theme: Introduce the person who died.

Series Scripture: *He heals the broken-hearted and binds up their wounds. Psalm 147:3.*

Scripture: Put scripture sticker here ➡
Isaiah 61:1b-2

Pray:
Lord Jesus, thank You for sending the Holy Spirit to comfort us. Thank You for giving us Kid Talk. Please comfort each child here today.

My <u>favorite</u> activity about this session:

☐ Meet My _____   ☐ TP Check -In   ☐ Acrostic for Decedent   ☐ Alphabet Poem

☐ Favorite Things   ☐ Paint Rocks   ☐ Happy Snaps   ☐ Snack – Ants On A Log

Explain your choice: _____

What I want to remember from this session: _____

_____

_____

_____
Signature

Is My Child's Grief Normal?

By Mel Erickson

Grief and mourning are our God-given healing responses to separation and loss. Therefore, the gamut of feelings and expressions of grief are necessary to the healing process. Each child's grief is unique to his or her personality, developmental stage, family dynamics and environmental stressors. (Just like adults. Yet, children grieve differently than adults do.) Let's look at some broad strokes of what you might see in a grieving child:

Regression
Changes in eating and sleeping pattern
Insecure or clingy
Nightmares
Difficulty concentrating
Afraid to be alone
Afraid of the dark
Cries more often
Headaches or stomachaches
Hyperactivity
Preoccupied with death and/or health
Speaks of decedent in present tense
Lack of emotions
Withdraws from friends
Takes on role of decedent
Irritable moods
Acting out or sassy
Suicidal thoughts
Fatigue or loss of energy
Angry towards parents or siblings
Non-compliance
Discipline problem in school
Guilt about words or actions
Magical thinking (unrealistic explanations)

It is important to notice the changes in a child and how long these changes persist. Note for example, a lot of a child's grief symptoms may mirror ADD and ADHD behaviors. Patient observation is needed as well as caring adult support.

Children are resilient and can handle almost anything as long as it is the truth and they are supported in love with lots of listening and comforting touch.

Truth telling builds a foundation of trust which is desirable to have as the teen years arrive. It is best that your child hears the truth from you and knows questions and discussion are always welcome. Use clear, simple language as much as possible to tell the story, then wait for the questions. The story will most likely be revealed in several small moments over time, such as driving in the car or bedtime. Expect repetition. It will probably take multiple reviews.

Remember 'normal' to grief is not ordinary normal. Everyone in the family is adjusting to a new normal. No one is the exact same person they were before the death. Consistency with the basics – mealtimes, bedtime and general ground rules of courtesy – provides some stability and continuity. Of course, this is easier said than done. It may be appropriate to have a friend or relative in the home who can help with this.

Kids remain kids, even when their hearts are broken. They do not sustain pain as long as adults can. They may be sobbing one minute and asking to go outside and play the next. Those short "teachable" moments are when we want to be a caring presence for a child. Again, this is not easy if you yourself are grieving. It helps to remember a child will grieve in small increments over time. His grief will recycle with sights, sounds, smells, and special occasions, just like an adult's. Additionally, he or she will undoubtedly recycle their grief in their teen years when their abstract thinking matures. The stories and memories will need to be revisited and made sense of. It is most helpful to have a memory book to trigger the buried emotions and grief responses. The more we can help a child express their grief in childhood, the less likely he or she will be to experience depression, rebellion, and risk-taking behaviors as a teen, known consequences of unresolved childhood grief.

Is your child's grief normal? Probably so. Extreme changes lasting over an extended period would be a flashing yellow light. Seek professional evaluation. Most "normal" grief responds to the support received from a children's grief group. Children may instinctively not want to add to their adult's emotional pain, so they do not talk. In a group they meet other kids who "get it." They learn they are not alone in experiencing the intense feelings and changes in themselves. They have repeated opportunities to express their feelings – good and bad – and tell their story. They overcome their fear of and resistance to the grieving process itself. They learn what they can do to help themselves feel better. At **Kid Talk**, we call it griefwork.

Kid Talk Lesson Plan – Week 3

Week 3: Funeral/Memorial   **See Leader's Guide for Details**

Scripture & Theme	Activities (minutes) OS = *Our Story* Memory Book LG – Leader's Guide	Handouts and Take-Home Griefwork

Psalm 46:1
God is our refuge and strength, an ever-present help in trouble.
 	
Pray:
God thank You for being our safe place and giving us strength. May each kid in our group know that You are always with us when we hurt.
 	
Theme:
We continue to show our love for the person who died. One way is a funeral or memorial service.
	OPEN: (Approximately **30** minutes)
	  Welcome: Ground Rules with poster
	  Psalm 147:3: ASL, discuss and pray.
	  Session Log: Psalm 46:1, discuss and pray.
	  Check-In with the Pop-Up-Pirate: when it pops, share from your Alphabet Poem or Favorite Things. Review **OS** Book completed pp. 6, 8, 9, 10, 12, 14 & 15. Apply stickers to all assigned pages.
	
	FOCUS: (Approximately **55** minutes)
	(30) **Funeral Story with Flannel Board**: *OS* p. 17 – While other children are creating their flannel board story, color a picture about the funeral on *OS* p. 17. Discuss these topics:
	  My Experience with Death: *OS* p. 15.
	  About the Death: *OS* p. 16.
	  Watermelon Hugs: *OS* p. 22. Read and discuss.
	Optional: make a butterfly and talk about how we will be transformed in heaven.
	(25) **Votive Battery Candles:** assemble the votive candle craft. Kids like to turn out the lights and read the "We Will Light Candles" poem and "We Remember Them" (*OS* pp. 18 and 19). You may choose to save this ritual for the CLOSE.
	
	SNACK: (Approximately **20** minutes)
	  Banana Caterpillars (seasonal choice)
	
	CLOSE: (Approximately **15** minutes)
	***Someday Heaven*:** read and discuss a question while children color butterflies.
	Chime Bell: Share "Happy Snaps" or create a ritual with votives and poems in *OS* pp. 18 and 19. See **LG.**
	Session Log
	Take-Home Griefwork
	Prayer
		Handouts for Adults:
		• *"Helping Children with Funerals"* and *"Helping Children Understand Cremation,"* both by Alan D. Wolfelt, Ph.D.
		• Watermelon Hugs
		
		Handouts for Kids:
		• *Our Story* binders
		• Session Logs
		• Bible Verse Stickers
		• Butterfly coloring pages
		
		Take-Home Griefwork:
		• Catch up on unfinished *OS* pp. 10, 12, 14, 15, 16
		• Discuss *OS* pp. 15 & 16 with adults
		
		Next Week:
		• Finish telling funeral stories on the flannel board.
		• Work on our Grief Bundle.
		• Make no-bake cookies.

NOTES

Check-In with Pop-Up-Pirate or Jack-in-the-Box: poke a sword in the barrel or crank three times, pass it on. When it goes off, that child shares from their griefwork about the funeral or about how their loved one died. (**OS** pp. 16 and 17. For variety, let that child choose the child who will share next.)

My Experience with Death: **OS** p. 15. This is a difficult page and may be emotionally loaded. Mister Rogers said making difficult matters mentionable is the best way to make them manageable. So, here we are together to talk about difficult matters. We ask that it be done as take-home griefwork so the child can process it with a close adult. Hopefully, the child has been told the truth about the death.

About the Death: **OS** p. 16. This is another difficult page that may also be very emotionally loaded. Again we ask it be done as take-home griefwork. Children can handle anything so long as it is the truth and they are supported in love. We encourage truth telling about the death because children are very intuitive and have listening ears. Not telling them the truth may create significant trust issues and close the door to communication in the teen years. We want home to be a place where we can safely talk about anything, because "we are in this together." This is the essence of the weekly memo/email for Week 3.

Funeral or Memorial Service: **OS** p. 17. A child may not know dates and locations. Therefore, it is sent home as take-home griefwork so an adult can help. In later years when grief will inevitably be recycling, this information may be helpful. It can help bring back memories and feelings that need to be worked through with more maturity.

Flannel Board: the children love creating a picture of their decedent's funeral or memorial service, or of a service they wish they had attended. At this point in time, creating a flannel board is at the facilitator's discretion. A flannel board and cut-out kits can be purchased or DIY instructions found on the internet. At some point in the future, we will publish the abstract patterns we use. This is an invaluable activity for a group or individual work with a grieving child.

Butterfly Coloring Pages: see **Kid Talk** Supply Pantry pp. 133 – 137.

Votive Battery Candles: each child receives a small votive battery candle, a small doily, and a square of colored construction paper of their choice. Purchased pre-cut neon colored shapes work also. Print the "We Will Light Candles" poem on Avery 5395 adhesive name labels. The poem can be stuck to the bottom side of the construction paper square.

Explain that lighting the candle is something you can do to "make your love visible" or a wordless "I love you," for the person who died. If someone in your family sees it, they will know you might like a hug. Ask the children when they are most likely to think about their decedent; what time of day or what day of the week do they think of them the most? Ask each child where he plans to keep his candle.

Bell Chime: the bell chime has a tone that lasts and lasts, symbolizing how far away we feel from our loved ones who are not here. Each child is invited to speak a message to the person who died and then send it off by tapping the bell. It is important to hold the bell until the tone has totally faded away before passing it to the next person. Symbolically, we want our message to travel the distance. The bell chime is another way we can "make our love visible" for the person who died. Our love does not turn off like a faucet. An important part of grieving is finding ways to express our love that still bubbles up when we are missing them. This is called memorializing. It is healthy griefwork.

Watermelon Hugs: *OS* p. 22. Read the poem to the children and ask if it would work as a "code" for them. This poem is also on a handout for the parents.

Snack: a Banana Caterpillar is made by slicing a banana into rounds and spreading each round with peanut butter or Nutella. (The URL below uses bananas and strawberries. Have fun!)

Add googly eyes or raisins for eyes. Poke pretzel sticks between the rounds for legs. Short pretzel pieces in the head work as antennae. Caterpillars work very hard to change life forms. We, too, will have a new life form in heaven that lasts for eternity when we have put our faith in Jesus Christ and choose to live for Him.

See www.sheknows.com/food-and-recipes/articles/990449/3-creepy-crawly-kids-snacks

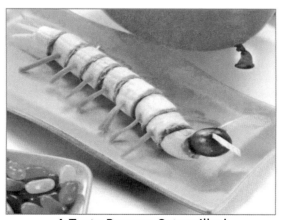
A Tasty Banana Caterpillar!

- Handouts for Parents/Guardians: "Helping Children with Funerals" and "Helping Children Understand Cremation" both by Alan D. Wolfelt, Ph.D., Watermelon Hugs
- Handouts for Kids: Session Logs and Bible Verse Stickers, Butterfly Coloring Pages
- Clipboard with Sign-In Sheet, pen and WELCOME sign
- Supplies to make name place cards for new arrivals
- **Our Story** binder
- Ground Rules poster
- Wilma, Pop-Up-Puppet
- Book: *'Someday Heaven'* by Larry Libby
- Glossary Cards from www.kidtalkgrief.com/ktbaccess
- Hand Sanitizer

- Plastic tablecloth for snack table - Pencils - Pens - Markers - Box of tissues - Basket of fiddle things (optional) - Pop-Up-Pirate or Jack-in-the-Box - Votive candles (battery), small doilies, 5" squares of colored paper, name tag labels printed with "We Will Light Candles" poem	- Extra copies of **OS** pp. 15, 16 and 17 - Butterfly craft (optional) - Bell Chime - Mandalas to color - Bead bracelet supplies or tickets (optional) - Snack supplies: Banana Caterpillars: bananas, strawberries, mini chocolate chips, small tube of frosting - Paper plates, plastic knives and napkins - Ice water and cups or hot water and hot chocolate

Room Set Up: set up an opening/closing table, a focus table and a snack table with a tablecloth to identify it easily. Also set up a supply table if possible.

Date: _____

Theme: We continue to show love for our decedents. An example is a funeral or memorial service.

Series Scripture: *He heals the broken-hearted and binds up their wounds. Psalm 147:3.*

Scripture: Put scripture sticker here ➡
Psalm 46:1

Pray:
God, thank You for being our safe place and giving us strength. May each kid in our group know that You are always with us when we hurt.

My <u>favorite</u> activity about this session:

☐ Scriptures   ☐ My Experience   ☐ About the Death   ☐ Flannel Board
                              With Death   Funeral Story

☐ Our 'Memorial'   ☐ Votive Candle   ☐ Watermelon Hugs   ☐ Snack - Banana
   with the Bell Chime   Caterpillars

Explain your choice: _____

_____

What I want to remember from this session: _____

_____

_____

Signature _____

Watermelon Hugs

Sometimes I'm sad;
I mean very-very sad.
Sometimes I'm mad;
I mean very-very mad.

Sometimes my feelings
Are in a jumbled-up way;
But my words get stuck
And I don't know what to say.

I need a secret word
That I can softly say
To let my people know
"I need some hugs today."

There's *flipper-flap* and *snipper-snap*
And *blueberry* and *baba-bee;*
But WATERMELON seemed just right—
It's the best secret word for me.

I shared my secret word with some
Special people--just a few---
So, when they hear WATERMELON,
They will know just what to do.

Now when I'm sad and want to hide
Under my fuzzy bear rug,
I just whisper WATERMELON,
And I get a great big HUG!

Carol Weedman Reed 2010 Printed by permission.

Week 4: My 'Grief Bundle'   **See Leader's Guide for Details**

Scripture & Theme	Activities (minutes) *OS* = *Our Story* Memory Book LG = Leader's Guide	Handouts and Take-Home Griefwork
Psalm 130:5 *and in His Word, I put my hope. I wait for the LORD, my whole being waits* **Pray:** Lord, help each of us to wait for You, to put our whole being and hope in You and in Your Word. **Theme:** My Grief Bundle has feelings attached.	**OPEN:** (Approximately **30** minutes) Early arrivals may do the Feelings Word Search or color. **Welcome:** Ground Rules with poster **Psalm 147:3** ASL, discuss and pray. **Session Log**: Psalm 130:5, discuss and pray. **Check-In:** Make a paperclip chain while sharing the Alphabet Poems. Ask, "When do you miss your decedent the most? What time of day is it?" Children may color the "Tangled Ball of Emotions" during conversation. **FOCUS:** (Approximately **55** minutes) Finish telling **funeral stories with flannel board.** (10) **Tangled Ball of Emotions Yarn Toss:** See **LG.** (10) **Grief Bundle:** *OS* p. 20. Use "Rainbow Mouth Coil" to explain the how we each have a grief bundle. Discuss. Children fill in their grief bundle. See **LG.** (10) **The Pain of Grief:** *OS* p. 21. See **LG.** (25) **Triangle Book:** This is a new way for each child to record their story. Drawing should be done before pasting the triangle pages together. Make sure that the pages are facing the same direction! See **LG.** **Feelings Word Search:** an optional activity. **SNACK:** (Approximately **20** minutes) Graham Cracker Band Aids. See **LG.** **CLOSE:** (Approximately **15** minutes) *Someday Heaven*: Select a question, read, and discuss. **Session Log** **Bead Bracelet** (optional) **Take-Home Griefwork** **Prayer**	**Handouts for Adults:** *"Helping Teenagers Cope with Grief"* by Alan D. Wolfelt, Ph.D. **Handouts for Kids:** • *Our Story* binders • Session Logs • Bible Verse Stickers • A Tangled Ball of Emotions • Feelings Word Search • Triangle Book Instructions **Take-Home Griefwork:** Share your triangle book with your family. **Next Week:** • Feelings Vase (magic!?) • Take more photos of our activities!

NOTES

Check-In with Paperclips: prepare a tray with a small paper cup for each child. Put 10 paperclips in each cup. Invite the children to make a paperclip chain for their "fiddle thing" during "Check In." This is a good precursor to the Grief Bundle exercise. It helps the children understand that grief attaches to grief.

Grief Bundle: *OS* p. 20. A 25' **rainbow mouth coil** can be purchased online. (See **Kid Talk** Supply Pantry pp. 133-137.) The leader explains how, "We each have a 'grief bundle.' Grief attaches to grief all the way back to the cradle. A little baby old enough to love and attach is old enough to grieve a major loss, even though they will not remember it. Grief from a new loss attaches to the grief of the most recent loss before it - like a paperclip chain. That's why we made paperclip chains for our fiddle things." Conceal the rainbow coil in one hand and slowly pull a small amount of the streamer out. Review your personal loss history from present to past, pulling out a length of streamer with each loss named. Losses include deaths (pets, too.), moves, changes or any losses the children may relate to. When you finish you have 25' feet of difficult-to-keep-in-your-hands and hard-to-contain streamer, a graphic visual of your collection of losses and feelings. Say, "It takes energy to contain all this emotion inside of us. This is energy that we need to think, play, study and be who we used to be.

The good news is that God heals our wounds. Remember Psalm 147:3? What does it remind us of? Yes, that God has given us the grieving process which helps us heal. There are also things that we can do to help manage this mess and help ourselves heal. We will talk more about these things next week and almost every week. We are going to look at the losses that may be in each of our grief bundles on p. 20 of *Our Story*. Another thing about our grief is that it 'recycles.' Let's read together what is says on p. 20. Have you ever had a grief attack? That is your grief recycling. It will recycle with the calendar, because your subconscious remembers. A lot of things may trigger your grief to recycle. For example: seeing another child with their parent if yours has died, having to play alone, smelling a fragrance that reminds you of your decedent, or hearing music that reminds you of that person. What other 'triggers' have brought on a 'grief attack' for you? Here is another important thing for you to know: your grief will recycle as you grow up, undoubtedly when you are a teenager. When it happens, look at your *Our Story* **Memory Book.** It will help you process your grief, i.e. do griefwork and heal."

Tangled Ball of Emotions: see handout on p. 59. "This looks a lot like our rainbow streamer bundle, doesn't it? Let's study the feelings in the bundle. Have you experienced any of them? Do different emotions make you think of different colors? What color might sad be? What about mad? Lonely?

Think about what feelings you experience and color them with the color of your choice. It will be interesting to see how our Ball of Emotions look after we've colored them. They will be different. Unique!" After the children have completed coloring their feelings of choice, note if the ball looks like a rainbow or a mud ball. (Someone might color it all dark colors.) Next week we'll do a "magic" activity that teaches us more about the feelings of grief.

Tangled Ball of Emotions Yarn Toss: is a large muscle activity that creates a visual of our tangled emotions. Stand in a circle. Standing around a table is helpful with younger kids. Name a feeling of grief, hold on to the end of the yarn and toss the ball across the circle for someone else to catch. (That is four things to remember: catch, hold the end of the yarn, name a feeling, and toss the yarn ball to another person.) Add another ball of yarn and have two going at the same time. If the kids are older, they may be able to keep three balls going. There is soon a lot of crisscrossed yarn to illustrate how complicated our feelings are. It's no wonder we feel like a mess when we are grieving. We are!

The Pain of Grief: *Our Story* p. 21. Purchase a box of small Band-Aids. Ask the children to color the child on p. 21 to look like themselves and then apply Band-Aids to the places on their drawing that illustrate where they feel their own grief. Invite the children to put their hands on their bodies to show where they feel the pain. Notice how we are the same and different. Discuss how our bodies are impacted by grief: trouble sleeping or eating, tired, tummy aches, difficulty breathing, heaviness in our chest or headaches to name some. Our immune system doesn't work as well when our grief is intense, so it is important to practice good health habits. Wash your hands a lot.

Triangle Book: this is a simple and unique way for the children to tell their story. Directions for how to fold and glue the pages are included with the curriculum material. We use pale shades of computer paper. We ask the kids to use at least three pages to draw and tell their decedent's story. Most of the kids have never seen a triangle book before and are intrigued with the mystery of how to open it and turn the pages. It really is very simple once you catch on. We pre-fold enough pages for all the children. The folded pages display nicely in a vertical napkin holder. This both saves time and benefits the younger children. Some children want to fold their own pages and are very capable of doing so. Color or write on the pages before gluing them together. Make sure that they all face the same direction e.g. that the bottom edges are lined up.

Graham Cracker Band Aids: www.kidfriendlythingstodo.com/. We like to make them with softened cream cheese and seedless raspberry jam. Yum!

- Handouts for Parents/Guardians: "Helping Teenagers Cope with Grief" by Alan
  D. Wolfelt, Ph.D.
- Handouts for Kids: Session Logs and Bible Verse Stickers, A Tangled Ball of Emotions, Feelings Word Search, Triangle Book Instructions
- Clipboard with Sign-In Sheet, pen and WELCOME sign
- Supplies to make name place cards for new arrivals
- ***Our Story*** binder
- Ground Rules poster
- Book: '*Someday Heaven*' by Larry Libby
- Glossary Cards from www.kidtalkgrief.com/ktbaccess

- Plastic tablecloth for Table 3
- Pencils
- Pens
- Markers
- Box of tissues
- Basket of fiddle things (optional)
- Box of paperclips: put 10 in a cup
- for each child.
- Rainbow Mouth Coil (Purchase
- online. (See **Kid Talk** Supply Pantry
- in Appendix).
- Hand Sanitizer

- Mandalas and coloring pages
- 8 ½" squares of light-colored computer paper tri-folded for triangle books, markers and glue sticks
- Bead bracelet supplies
- Snack supplies for Graham Cracker Band Aids: graham crackers cut squares into 1" strips, softened cream cheese, seedless raspberry jam
- Paper plates, plastic knives and napkins
- Ice water and cups or hot water and hot chocolate

Room Set Up: We cover the snack table with a plastic cloth for this session.

Kid Talk Session Log – Week 4

Date: _____

Theme: My grief bundle has feelings attached.

Series Scripture: *He heals the broken-hearted and binds up their wounds. Psalm 147:3.*

Scripture: Put scripture sticker here ➡
Psalm 130:5

Pray:
Lord, help each of us to wait
for You, to put our whole being and
hope in You and in Your Word.

My <u>favorite</u> activity about this session:

☐ Scriptures   ☐ Feelings Word   ☐ Flannel Board   ☐ Grief Bundle
                           Search   Funeral Story

☐ Triangle Book   ☐ Tangled Ball of   ☐ The Pain of Grief   ☐ Snack – Graham
                           Emotions   Cracker Band Aids

Explain your choice: _____

_____

What I want to remember from this session: _____

_____

_____

Signature _____

Feelings of Grief Word Search - Activity

Circle **ten** different feelings hidden in this puzzle: love, sad, mad, confused, lonely, guilty, relief, shock, afraid, jealous. My feelings are unique to me so I have circled them (again) with a different color.

GRIEF... A Tangled "Ball' of Emotions - Activity

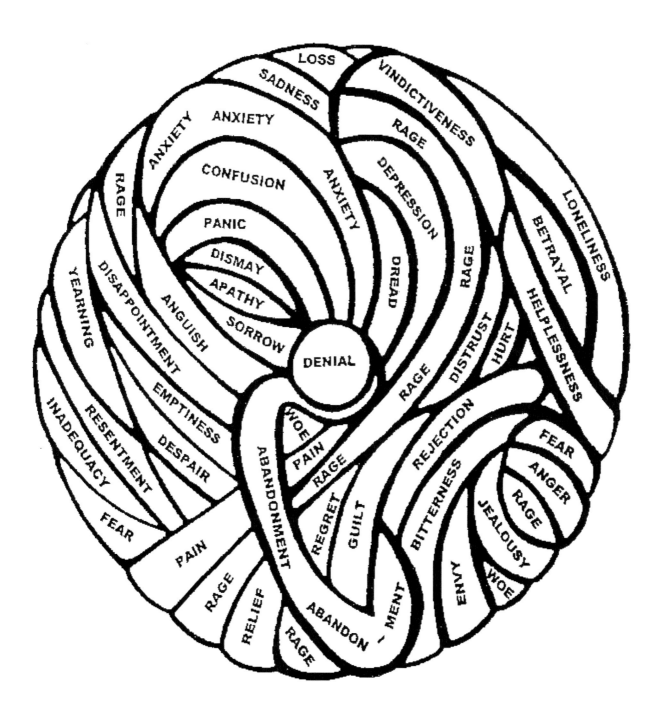

Used with Permission of Dr. H. Norman Wright.

www.hnormanwright.com

59

1. The triangle book is made by squaring off 8 ½" x 11" paper to 8 ½" squares. At a corner fold the edges to meet and crease. Trim off the extra strip with scissors.
2. Each square page is folded diagonally corner-to-corner in both directions. Consider this side A.
3. Flip the paper over (to side B) and fold it in half. The result is that the crests of the diagonal folds are on the opposite side of the half fold.
4. With the crest folds facing up, push the half fold to meet in the middle, resulting in a triangle shape that opens into a square.
5. After drawing and/or writing on the desired number of pages on Side B, the triangles are glued together to make a triangle shaped book. Be careful to open each page before gluing to the next page in order to make sure that the bottom of the picture/story is lined up with the bottom of the next page.

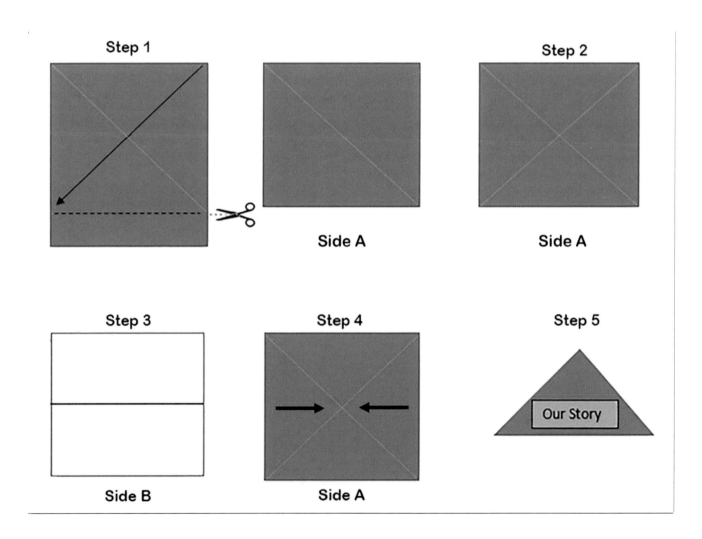

Kid Talk Lesson Plan – Week 5

Week 5: Feelings of Grief

See Leader's Guide for Details

Scripture & Theme	Activities (minutes) OS = *Our Story* Memory Book LG = Leader's Guide	Handouts and Take-Home Griefwork
Psalm 34:18 *The LORD is close to the broken-hearted and saves those who are crushed in spirit.* **Pray:** Lord, thank You for wanting to be close to each of us. We are broken hearted. Please comfort us as our spirits are crushed by grief. **Theme:** It's OK to have many different feelings of grief.	**OPEN:** (Approximately **30** minutes) **Welcome:** Ground Rules with poster **Psalm 147:3:** ASL, discuss and pray. **Session Log:** Psalm 34:18, discuss and pray. **Check-In:** Give a weather report that describes how you are doing. For example, "mostly sunny" or "grey skies" or "stormy" etc. Does the weather affect your feelings? **(10) Snack Preparation:** Mix no-bake cookies that need to refrigerate. **FOCUS:** (Approximately **55** minutes) **(35) Feelings Vase:** *OS* p. 23. Take a photo of each child holding their feelings card(s) to demonstrate that feeling. If time does not allow for doing "Grief Tips," save the vase with "yucky" water for next week. **(5) Watermelon Hugs:** *OS* p. 22. Read the poem. Can we use "watermelon" as a code here at **Kid Talk**? Review Week 3 **LG**. **(15) Grief Behaviors:** *OS* p. 24. It is important to note the difference between the behaviors of grief and intentional griefwork. (Griefwork: *OS* p. 26). Both are mourning behaviors and contribute to our healing. Which do we want to do? Why? See **LG**. **SNACK:** (Approximately **10** minutes) Cookies and milk! What does it mean to have "raw" feelings? See **LG** and Supply List. **CLOSE:** (Approximately **15** minutes) **Session Log** *Someday Heaven:* **Read and discuss one question.** **Take-Home Griefwork** **Prayer**	**Handouts for Adults:** • *"Grief Tips for Kids and Teens"* • *"Sibling Survivor Guilt"* by Bob Baugher, Ph.D. **Handouts for Kids:** • *Our Story* binder • Session Logs • Bible Verse Stickers • *"Grief Tips for Kids and Teens"* • No-Bake Cookie recipe **Take-Home Griefwork:** Talk to family about what feelings or behaviors of grief surprise you. **Next Week:** We discover the magic of clearing up the "yucky feelings." We will talk about things we can do to help ourselves feel better. We will talk more about anger and guilt. We will pop popcorn without a lid!

NOTES

The Feelings Vase: this activity has profound impact and is a favorite.

Materials Needed:

- 32 "Feelings Cards" (Printable PDF at www.kidtalkgrief.com/ktbaccess Print and laminate them.)
- Clear glass bud vase with a bulb at the base, add water, level with the top of the bulb with a drop of food coloring
- Set of liquid food colors
- Container of small pearlescent floral stones
- Small container lid to use as a "tray" for the food colors. It makes it easier to pass them around
- Individual laminated cards with a "Grief Tip for Kids" on each one or a printed list for each child

1. Distribute the feelings cards around the room or over a table. Invite the children to "shop" for 2 or 3 feelings that match how their grief feels. No worries if someone else wants the same card. We will all be sharing them.

2. Settle at the table and have the children turn to **Our Story** p. 23 to record their own feelings with words or pictures. Demonstrate with a feeling card of your own (leader) how we will proceed. Hold up the feeling card and say, "I have chosen love because I will always love my dad." Then select a color of food coloring (red, yellow, blue, or green) to represent the feeling and say, "for me, love is red." Squeeze one drop of red into the bud vase. Then ask, "Is there anyone who would like to share LOVE with me?" (The children will begin to pose this question to the others.) Go around the table to give everyone the opportunity to "own" love, tell why AND name the color it is for them. The person to first share a feeling puts the food color into the vase for everyone else. The leader might ask the person to demonstrate love for a photo – or ask the whole group – and take a photo. Alternatively explain that everyone will pick one of their feelings to act out for a photo when we've finished going around the table. It seems to be most efficient to have each child share about all the feeling cards that they have chosen. When done, pass along the vase and the little tray of food colors to the person on the left.

3. It doesn't take long for the water in the vase to change colors. It will eventually turn very dark and murky or "yucky." Explain that, "Yucky is how we feel inside when our heart is broken because someone important to us has died. Think about the mixture of feelings: both good and bad ones all in there together. It can make us feel a little crazy or even be frightened because we have never felt like this before."

4. Say, "It takes energy to cope with the stress of all that yucky stuff going on inside us. Next, we will discover what we can do to help ourselves feel better. (GRIEFWORK!) (We may need to save the vase in a safe place until next week.) I need to tell you that the water will never be clear again – just like we'll never be quite the same again. But there are things that we can do to help ourselves feel less bad or even lots better. God has given us the healing that comes through doing griefwork."

5. A contact lens cleaning solution squeeze bottle with the label removed which contains bleach* is perfect for the "magic" portion of this activity. Ask the children what bleach can do as a reminder to be very careful. Demonstrate the technique of tipping and squirting bleach into the vase AFTER naming something that you can do to help yourself feel better. *This is griefwork.* This is a good time to remember that, "God is always with us and has given us this grieving process to help us heal. He is also *right there with us* to comfort us and help us make good decisions about how to deal with our emotional pain." Use the "Grief Tips for Kids" handout or cards as clues for griefwork we can choose to do.

    *For safety, only the facilitator should handle the bottle with bleach.

6. At some point comment, "It sure takes a lot of bleach to change the color! We are working hard at doing things that help us heal. What is that called again? Oh, yes! Griefwork!" Suggest that the children look at their handout, "Grief Tips for Kids and Teens." It's a great springboard for conversation. As we continue naming griefwork and adding bleach, the water begins to lighten. Explain, "As the vase sits over time, it continues to get lighter, however time alone does not heal. Time may help us distance a little from the pain of grief. The truth is that 'healing' or 'grieving clean' does not just happen without the hard work of grief. The good news is: instead of feeling 'yucky,' we can feel less pain or even feel good." An amazing amount of grief AND emotions get safely expressed while doing this exercise. It really is powerful, interactive, and fun.

7. Finally, and this portion of the activity often carries over to the next session, we will add "treasured memories" to the vase. After a week the solution has probably become a pale yellow, but not clear, emphasizing how we will never be quite the same again. A basket or container of floral stones is passed around.

8. The facilitator demonstrates how to take a stone, share the "treasured memory" that it represents, and then drop the stone into the vase. The stones raise the water level. When the water gets close to the top of the vase, it is time to stop. Every child should get at least two opportunities to share a treasured memory. Close with the words, "Even though our loved ones are no longer here with us, our memories of them fill us."

Watermelon Hugs: *Our Story* p. 22. Revisit this poem. It offers a codeword for when we might need a hug: "watermelon." Have someone read it. Ask, "Do you have to be young to need a 'Watermelon Hug?'" No! "Would this code work at your house? Will it work for us here at **Kid Talk**?" (Yep!)

Grief Behaviors: *Our Story* pp. 24 & 26. Explain that, "The behaviors of grief are when our grief is expressed in our actions. Examples are crying, wailing, flying off the handle, feeling too sad to do anything, having a stomachache, talking about the person who died or putting flowers on the grave. Grief behaviors are also called 'mourning.' 'Griefwork' is also mourning, except we <u>choose</u> to do it, knowing that it will help us move through our grief. So, looking at our list on p. 24, which behavior is griefwork? (Crying, talking about the decedent, and putting flowers on the grave.) Sometimes grief behavior can spew out of us and we call it 'grief vomit.' We'll talk more about that next week. For now, let's remember grief behaviors are normal, but we do not want to hurt ourselves or anyone we love because we are heartbroken. We have other choices. Your handout tonight, 'Grief Tips for Kids and Teens' lists two pages of things you can do that are griefwork. We are going to talk about them a lot."

No-Bake Cookies: these cookies are mixed with gloved hands. They have been called "aggression cookies." Everyone participates by adding ingredients and mixing. The recipe is included on the Supply List and is printed as a handout. The cookies need to be refrigerated, so we make them first after OPENING. Have zip lock baggies on hand for taking cookies home to share – maybe. Milk and cookies just go together as comfort food. Serve water also, in case of allergies.

- Handouts for Parents/Guardians: "Grief Tips for Kids and Teens." "Sibling Survivor Guilt" by Bob Baugher, Ph.D.
- Handouts for Kids: Session Logs and Bible Verse Stickers, No-Bake Cookie Recipe, and "Grief Tips for Kids and Teens"
- Clipboard with Sign-In Sheet, pen and WELCOME sign
- Supplies to make a name place card for new arrivals
- ***Our Story*** binder
- Ground Rules poster
- Book: '*Someday Heaven*' by Larry Libby
- Glossary Cards from www.kidtalkgrief.com/ktbaccess
- Hand Sanitizer

- Plastic tablecloth for Table 3
- Pencils
- Pens
- Markers
- Box of tissues
- For the Feelings Vase Exercise, you will need:
  - Clear glass flower vase with a bulb shaped base
  - Water to fill the bottom of the vase with a drop of blue food coloring in it so that it shows up
  - Red, blue, yellow and green liquid food coloring on a small tray or lid for passing around
  - 32 stick figure feelings cards (See **Kid Talk** Supply Pantry in Appendix.)
  - Floral stones in a container with a lid. We use this container lid as the food coloring "tray" and store the food coloring in the same container.
  - Contact lens solution squeeze bottle filled with bleach

- Paper Towels
- Mandalas and coloring sheets
- Ingredients and utensils for making No-Bake Cookies:
  - ¾ C peanut butter
  - ½ C honey
  - 1 tsp vanilla
  - 2 C oats
  - 1 C Rice Krispies
  - 1 C mini chocolate chips
  - ½ tsp cinnamon (optional)

  Mix together with gloved hands and shape into walnut- sized balls. A #24 cookie scoop makes even portions easy. Refrigerate one hour to "set."

- Zip lock baggies for taking cookies home
- Bead bracelet supplies or tickets (optional)
- Cups, napkins, ice water and milk

Room Set Up: cover the snack table with a plastic cloth for this session

Kid Talk Session Log - Week 5

Date: _____

Theme: It is OK to have many feelings of grief.

Series Scripture: *He heals the broken-hearted and binds up their wounds. Psalm 147:3.*

Scripture: Put scripture sticker here ➡
Psalm 34:18

Pray:
Lord, thank You for wanting to be close to each of us. We are brokenhearted. Please comfort us as our spirits are crushed by grief.

My <u>favorite</u> activity about this session:

☐ Scriptures   ☐ Weather Check-In   ☐ Feelings Vase   ☐ Watermelon Hugs

☐ Behaviors of Grief   ☐ *Someday Heaven*   ☐ Snack – No- Bake Cookies

Explain your choice: _____

_____

What I want to remember from this session: _____

_____

_____

Signature _____

¾ C. peanut butter

½ C. honey

1 tsp. vanilla

2 C. oats

1 C. Rice Krispies

1 C. mini chocolate chips

½ tsp. cinnamon (optional)

Mix thoroughly. Roll into walnut-size portions*

Place on wax paper and refrigerate for one hour.

*Use a #24 Cookie Scoop for easy portions.

Here is a list of ideas to help you when you are grieving the death of a loved one. You may find some of these suggestions helpful, and you may think of even better ideas on your own. There are many ways to move toward healing and to remember your loved one.

Talk with a Friend

Consider talking with a friend, sharing your thoughts and feelings about your loved one's death, as well as memories of this special person. Choose someone you can trust to respect your feelings and who will not tell others what you have said. You may find it hard to open up with another person, but it eventually can help you feel better.

Carry or Wear a Linking Object

Carry something special that reminds you of the one who has died. It could be jewelry or another small object. Choose something that will fit in your pocket or school bag.

Create a Memory Book

Gather pictures of your loved one and other keepsakes, such as artwork or an event program. Glue these to pieces of paper to make a scrapbook. You can be creative in the type of paper you choose and the way you bind the pages together. You may then look through this keepsake by yourself or with others.

Remember Your Dreams

After a loved one has died, you might dream about that person. Some dreams may be weird or scary; others may be happy and fun. No matter which type of dream you have, it can be helpful to talk about it with someone you trust.

Tell Others What Helps You and What Doesn't

It may be hard to tell others what you need, but it is important. After all, others cannot read your mind. So, tell a trusted adult friend or family member what makes you sad and what makes you feel better. Also find out what helps others who are grieving because it is different for each person.

Plant Something as a Memorial

Consider planting a tree or flowers in memory of your loved one - something special that you take care of and enjoy. You may want to plant it near your home, so that you can watch it grow and change.

Spend Time in your Loved One's Space

You may find it comforting to sit in your loved one's favorite chair or to stand in his or her room for a short time. Only do this if and when it feels OK (but remember, feeling OK can include letting out healing tears.)

Read Bible Verses That Remind You of Who God Is

The better we know God from the Bible, the easier it is to trust Him when life is hard and unfair. Scripture reminds you of how much He loves you, will comfort you and provide for you. Talk to Him anytime and often. (Pray!)

Sleep with Something Soft

No one is ever too old to cuddle with a soft toy or pillow. You might find one that in some way reminds you of your loved one. You may even have a toy or pillow that belonged to the person who died. Another idea is to sleep in one of your loved one's shirts.

Write Your Loved One a Letter

Write a letter or other messages to your loved one. Include your thoughts and feelings. You also can write about activities you used to do together. Write it on your computer or handwrite it on special paper. Keep these letters or throw them away - you get to decide what you do with them.

Light a Candle

Consider lighting a battery candle in memory of your loved one. This can be especially meaningful with a group of people. As you light the candle, say your loved one's name or something special about him or her. Remember, ONLY LIGHT "real" CANDLES WHEN YOU ARE SUPERVISED BY AN ADULT. You can use a battery candle to safely leave a "love light" burning.

Use Your Hands

Actively using your hands can help you feel better. This may include putting together puzzles, painting, working with clay, or even helping others with chores or cleaning. Create something that would make your decedent smile.

Listen to Music

Sometimes music can remind you of your loved one and you may feel sad, especially when you hear a certain song. Music can help you cry when you need to cry. You also can choose music that makes you feel good. You may want to start your day by listening to a favorite song.

Remember, it is OK to Laugh

Funny things can happen to you, just like they did before your loved one died. Take time to listen to or tell a funny joke. It's OK to laugh. It can make you feel better, just like crying does.

Remember, it is OK to Cry

Sometimes when you miss your loved one a lot you might start to cry. During this time, you may want to be alone or you may want to be with others. Do what is best for you

Help Someone Else

You may meet other kids who have also had a loved one die. You can reach out and be a good friend to them by listening or inviting them to play. You also may be able to do practical things for them, like help them with homework or a chore that they don't have energy to do. Another way to help others is by doing fundraising or other activities to help people who are grieving a loss.

Find a Kids' Grief Support Group

It really helps to process your grief with other kids who "get it." Ask your parent to look for (or request) a "**Kid Talk**" group by talking to your pastor or school counselor. Visit www.kidtalkgrief.com to learn how to start and conduct a group.

Adapted from 'Grief Tips' by James Miller, with kind permission.
www.shop.willowgreen.com

Acclaimed writer and photographer, James E. Miller created Willowgreen Inc. in 1986 to help people deal effectively with life's momentous transitions.
He melds the written and spoken word with photography and music in ways that inform, encourage, and inspire the whole person.

Sibling Survivor Guilt

Bob Baugher, Ph.D.

We know that guilt is a part of the human condition; and it is certainly part of most people's bereavement process. If you experienced survivor guilt when your brother or sister died, join the crowd. Let's look at some of the common types:

Being alive: Knowing that your brother or sister will never experience life again while you continue to live day after day may bring guilt feelings. It's not that you can't understand why your sibling's life was cut short and you continue to live.

Surpassing the age he/she was: Survivor guilt can rear its ugly head when you reach and surpass the age to which your sibling lived…. And every day you live beyond that date may somehow feel strange, unfair, or even a relief….

Using his things: For some bereaved siblings, using items that belonged to their deceased brother or sister brings comfort and produces feelings of closeness. Others report that using items brings feelings of unworthiness…. When an item inevitably wears out or becomes unusable, you may feel badly that yet another piece of your brother or sister has faded from use. Other people may not understand this significance….

Doing things he/she never got a chance to do: This is a quite common source of survivor guilt and it becomes especially poignant when you see the look on your parents' face that says, "I wish your brother/sister could have done this or been here for this"….

Experiencing pleasure: Here you are enjoying yourself at a party, on vacation, at the beach, the movies, or out to dinner and suddenly it hits you—"How can I be having fun like this when she can never do this again?" Friends may notice your sudden change of mood, but you may not want to tell them for fear of spoiling their fun.

Seeing your loved ones cry: One of the most difficult aspects of death is watching those around you grieve the loss and realizing there is not much you can do to ease their pain. You may have had the awkward experience of standing there and having the desire to say, "Hey, I'm still here!"…You feel guilty for standing there, being alive, and realizing your existence has little effect on easing your loved ones grief…..

Taking risks you shouldn't: If you are or were a normal adolescent, you engaged in activities you knew were unsafe. However, because of your brother or sister's death, you also know better than most of your friends that a young person can die and leave their family devastated. Yet, there you were, taking risks and feeling guilt as a result…..

Feeling like it should have been you: This is another common one, especially when you are feeling down on yourself o when your parents have criticized you…..If you are having thoughts such as these it is very important that you call a friend, a counselor, your parents, the crisis center, or some other person who can listen to you. These are thoughts that may indicate you are depressed……

Not doing enough to keep his memory alive: Here you are going through the course of your day, when it hits you that you have not been thinking of him/her. Or you find that you aren't remembering some of the ways he did things.

Then you kick yourself for "forgetting". Do you realize that you will never forget your brother or sister? One way to help with is guilt issue is to begin writing down all your memories. If you're not a writer, then talk into a tape recorder... It's a great way to ease this aspect of survivor guilt: stories are the way we best remember...

Before I get to the last type of survivor guilt, I want to offer some ways that you might ease some of your guilt:

> **1.** Go back through the list and circle the ones that are relevant to you.

> **2.** Find someone who will be a good listener and not judge you. Tell this person that you wish to talk about some guilt that you have been feeling around your brother/sister's death. Most importantly tell this person that you want them to listen without trying to "fix" it, and without saying, "don't feel guilt." You simply want someone who will listen. There is something positive about "getting out" your guilt feelings and not letting them eat away at your insides.

> **3.** Next, focus on the positive. Tell your friend all the good things you've done since your sibling died. Don't be modest. Omit the term "I should have" from your vocabulary because you can <u>never</u> fix the past. You can only work on the present.

> **4.** Ask yourself the following question: "What would it take to forgive myself?" And do something to work on this.

Not living up to his standards: Someone said it well years ago, "The dead have it easy-we are reluctant to say bad things about them and, unlike us, they make no further mistakes in their life." In other words, your brother/sister was a hard act to follow. So, you feel more guilt because you are not this ideal person. Your challenge is to live up to <u>your own</u> realistic standards and allow yourself to make mistakes. A good method to follow the next time you make a "stupid" mistake is to say, "What would I say right now if my best friend made the exact same mistake?" And then say that exact thing to yourself. I challenge you to treat yourself as well as you would your best friend. Besides, I bet that's what your brother or sister would want for you. Don't you agree?

You need not walk alone...

'Sibling Survivor Guilt' originally published in The Compassionate Friends Magazine: <u>We Need Not Walk Alone</u>, Summer, 1998, pp.15, 17.

Highline Community College Des Moines, Washington

bbaugher@highline.edu
www.bobbaugher.com

Kid Talk Lesson Plan – Week 6

Week 6: Anger and Guilt
See Leader's Guide for Details

Scripture & Theme	Activities (minutes) OS = *Our Story* Memory Book LG = Leader's Guide	Handouts and Take-Home Griefwork
<u>Deuteronomy 29:29a</u> *The secret things belong to the Lord our God.* **Pray:** Lord, please help each grieving person here today to trust YOU with the things they do not understand – the secret things. Help us to trust You as Lord. **Theme:** Anger and guilt are a normal part of kids' grief. What can we do with these feelings?	**OPEN: (30 minutes)** <u>Welcome</u>: Ground Rules with poster <u>Psalm 147:3</u>: ASL, discuss and pray. <u>Session Log</u>: Deuteronomy 29:29a, discuss and pray. <u>Check-in</u>: Volcano of Feelings – Color and talk. How is your volcano of feelings? **FOCUS: (60 minutes)** **(10)** <u>Feelings Vase Review</u>: Pick up where you left off. Add floral stones and treasured memories or save this activity for the CLOSE. **(5)** <u>Anger Thermometer</u>: See **LG.** **(5)** <u>Toilet Bowl Love</u>: *OS* p. 25. See **LG.** **(10)** <u>Grief Vomit Bags</u>: Anger and guilt are the "loudest" and most difficult feelings to manage. Talk about how to use the grief vomit bag and "unlimited take-backs." **(5)** <u>Persian Petition for Reconciliation</u>: Discuss guilt and how we can deal with it. Read the poem together. **(20)** <u>Scream Boxes</u>: Anger is not wrong. What we do with it may be. A scream box is a good way to let off steam without hurting anyone or ourselves. See **LG.** **SNACK: (20 minutes)** <u>Popcorn</u> with no lid on the popper. (Refer to **LG**) Anger can pop out! How can we take charge of it? What can we do with it? **CLOSE: (15 minutes)** *Someday Heaven:* Read and discuss one question. <u>Session Log</u> <u>Take-Home Griefwork</u> – Apply stickers to pages that have been assigned. <u>Treasured Memories</u> with iridescent floral stones <u>Prayer</u>	**Handouts for Adults:** Anger Thermometer **Handouts for Kids:** • *Our Story* Binders • Anger Thermometer • Session Logs • Bible Verse Stickers • Volcano of Feelings • Persian Petition for Reconciliation **Take-Home Griefwork:** • Review *OS* pp. 24, 25 and 26 with your family. • Talk about "grief vomit," saying "ouch!" and "unlimited take-backs." • Remember "Watermelon Hugs." **Next Week:** We will shoot marshmallows and make bumper stickers.

NOTES

Check-In with Volcano of Feelings: color this illustration and talk about the feelings of grief that may build pressure and "gush" out. Have the children identify which feelings they recognize in themselves and color them. Refer to the Anger Thermometer to learn to recognize how anger builds. Talk about guilt and how our head and our heart may not agree. It is important that we "give ourselves a fair trial." Watch for magical thinking in the children. A child may create an explanation for an event that just is not true. This is one of the reasons it is so important for children to know the truth about a death.

Anger Thermometer: consider saying, "Anger is sneaky. Sometimes we do not know why we feel disgruntled or upset. Notice that anger often starts with fear or worry. When someone dies, we wonder who else will die? We may worry about, "Who will love me?" or "Who will take care of me?" These questions and fears are normal for kids AND adults. It is important to talk about them with someone we trust and with God. If we can resolve our fears early on, it is less likely we will get out of control. Remember, anger is a feeling and it is not wrong. What we DO with it is what matters. Jesus got angry in the temple at all the money-making activity. He stated the problem and acted without hurting anyone or himself. He is our role model. Let's talk about our anger and what we can do with it. Remember Mr. Rogers' quote: Making difficult matters mentionable is the best way to make them manageable."

Grief Vomit Bags: suggested narrative – "Remember the volcano? Sometimes our emotions, prompted by grief, just blurt out in unkind words or behaviors. OOPS! A good family ground rule is 'unlimited take-backs' and 'labeling grief vomit' for a year or so after the death. For example: Let's say that I point my loaded (verbal) gun at you and yell, 'You never….!' or 'You always….!' or 'I hate….!' In response you say, 'OUCH!' (That is all.) Then I say, 'Oops! That was grief vomit. (Labeled it.) May I take it back?' Your answer is, 'Yes! Want to talk?' Remember: OUCH! Label it. And unlimited take-backs." It is helpful to explain this to parents in an email or written memo.

Feelings Vase Review: invite the children to retrieve the feelings cards they chose last week. Review which feelings we shared with each other. (The leader may want to add a feeling or two that has not been chosen i.e. love, anger, guilt, worry, jealous.) It is important to talk about these feelings as natural to grief. For example, "love doesn't turn off like a faucet. We continue to feel love for the person who has died, and it is important to find ways to express it or make it visible. This is memorializing. It is healthy griefwork. It is natural to worry about who else might die or even think about our own death." Make sure the children have recorded their own feelings on *Our Story* p. 23. Review the "Grief

Tips for Kids and Teens" handout, naming things that we can do to feel better e.g. "griefwork." Each child names a "griefwork" activity or a "stress management choice" and then squirts bleach into the vase. (Use your judgement re: the maturity of your group to decide if the children can squirt the bleach or a leader should do it. Safety is imperative.) *Note: Grief is a form of stress, so stress management techniques – like deep breathing – help. However, "griefwork" is very specific to the stress of grief. It is also mourning behavior.* After a **lot** of "griefwork" squirts of bleach, the dark water begins to lighten up. It will never get totally clear; just like we will never be the same after someone important to us dies. The water **will** become a pale yellow. If we leave it for a week, it will lighten up a little more demonstrating how **time does help but time alone does not heal**.

This is important to understand. We, kids and adults alike, want to intentionally choose to do the work of grief in order to feel better and help ourselves move forward through the grieving process.

Toilet Bowl Love: *OS* p. 25. Suggested narrative: "People say and do things that hurt us, especially when we are extra sensitive because of our grief. What happens to a toilet that is not flushed? It gets yucky. So, do we - if we cannot let go of our pain and anger. Forgiveness is an important component of healing our grief. With God's help we can flush away hurtful words and actions as many times as necessary. We don't forget like God does. We need to flush again every time the hurt comes back. The good news is, we can." Give examples of hurtful things that have been said or done that may hurt such as, 'I know just how you feel, my dog died.' Or 'Your grandpa was old. Who cares?' Ask children to share. They can pass around the mechanical toilet that flushes, if you have one. Have them write on the lines going into the toilet on *OS* p. 25 what they are choosing to flush. We can always go into the bathroom, speak into the real toilet and flush what needs to go. It will help us let go of the hurt, anger, and potential bitterness.

Persian Petition for Reconciliation: this is a good prayer to read together out loud after discussing guilt. Explain that, "Guilt is often a part of the in the grieving process for adults and especially for children who are prone to magical thinking. Guilt might be framed by thoughts that begin with, 'If only……, I should have, could have, would have… ' Our head and our heart may not be in sync. We may cognitively know that we did our best at the time, in the circumstances, with what we knew, but our hearts say, 'Yes, but if only….' Magical thinking makes this even more complicated." For example, one child stated, "If I hadn't argued with my dad that morning, he wouldn't have had a heart attack." It is important to carefully and thoroughly explore magical thinking and shed the light of truth on it. It takes gentle reinforcement.

Scream Boxes: materials needed for each child are a shoe box with a lid, a paper towel tube (or similar length of heavy cardboard tube such as from gift wrap), **lots** of newspapers and colorful duct tape. Pre-cut a sunburst in the middle of one short end of the box. Poke the tube through about ⅔ of the way. Wad up half sheets of newspaper as tightly as possible and stuff them very tightly into the box all around the tube. The more newspaper, the better the insulation. When it gets to the point that you need help to hold the lid down, duct tape it closed. It takes two people: one to hold and one to tape. Cover every edge where air or sound could "leak out" with duct tape, including the tube. If done well, you can scream into the tube and hear only a little squeak. It works.

Pop Popcorn with No Lid: an air popper works. We use a West Bend Stir Crazy Popcorn Maker for broader distribution of the popcorn. Place the popper on a large sheet or tablecloth that is no longer needed. It may get oil stained. Heat a small amount of oil, ask a child to pour in the half cup of popcorn and stand back. The kernels are **extremely hot** when they pop out, so safety precautions are essential. We make protective "bibs" out of plastic grocery sacks to shield the children's clothing. Protective goggles are essential and add to the fun. This becomes a time of shrieks and laughter as kids try and catch popcorn in their bowls. It takes several batches to pop enough corn for all the kids to fill their paper bowls – not necessarily their appetites. Have a salt-shaker handy. We like to serve apples or apple juice with the popcorn. The kids enjoy cutting the apples with the corer and wedge cutting kitchen tool. Ask the children what they think our snack has to do with anger and guilt that we've been talking about. What does it have to do with Grief Vomit? What can it help us remember to do when our emotions "pop?" (Grief Vomit, Ouch! And Unlimited Take-backs.)

Safety Note: We always advise caution and extreme care when handling bleach or working with hot materials. It is the responsibility of the facilitator(s) to ensure the children's safety and well-being at all times during the sessions. Please ensure you take all possible steps to protect everyone from hot oil and hot popcorn by using eye, skin and clothes protection, and our recommendation is that **only facilitators should handle the containers with bleach.**

- Handouts for Parents/Guardians: Anger Thermometer
- Handouts for Kids: "Volcano," "Anger Thermometer," "Persian Petition for Reconciliation Prayer," Session Log and Bible Verse Stickers
- Clipboard with Sign-In Sheet, pen and WELCOME sign
- Supplies to make a name place card for new arrivals
- ***Our Story*** binder
- Ground Rules poster
- Book: '*Someday Heaven*' and box with question cards
- Glossary Cards from www.kidtalkgrief.com/ktbaccess
- Hand Sanitizer

- Sheet or plastic tablecloth for floor - Pencils - Pens - Markers - Box of tissues - Basket of fiddle things (optional) - Toilet Bowl Magnet (toy that "flushes") - Scream box supplies: a shoe box for each child with a sunburst- shaped hole cut in the middle of a narrow end, a paper towel tube, lots of newspapers and colored duct tape - Paper bag (lunch sack) for each child to make a "Grief Vomit" Bag. Talk about Grief Vomit and saying "ouch" and unlimited "take backs."	- Feelings Vase that was saved from last week, squirt bottle of bleach and pearly floral stones to represent precious memories - Basket of laminated "Grief Tips for Kids" cards - Mandalas and coloring sheets - Make a "bib" for each child from a plastic grocery bag. It will protect their clothing from the hot popcorn splatter. - Protective glasses/eyewear for popcorn activity - Snack: Pop Corn Popper, a small amount of coconut oil, popcorn, salt, a paper bowl for each child, apples, an apple corer/wedger tool, a cutting board, napkins, cups and water.

Room Set Up: use a heavy plastic or cloth tablecloth under the popcorn popper.

Kid Talk Session Log - Week 6

Date: _____

Theme: Anger and guilt are a normal part of kids' grief. What can we do with these feelings?

Series Scripture: *He heals the broken-hearted and binds up their wounds. Psalm 147:3.*

Scripture: Put scripture sticker here ➡
Deuteronomy 29:29a

Pray:
Lord, please help each grieving person here today to trust YOU with the things they do not understand – the secret things. Help us to trust You as Lord.

My <u>favorite</u> activity about this session:

☐ Volcano of Feelings   ☐ Grief Tips   ☐ Toilet Bowl Love   ☐ Grief Vomit Bags

☐ Persian Petition of Reconciliation   ☐ Scream Boxes   ☐ *Someday Heaven*   ☐ Snack -Popcorn Without a Lid!

Explain your choice: _____

_____

What I want to remember from this session: _____

_____

_____

Signature _____

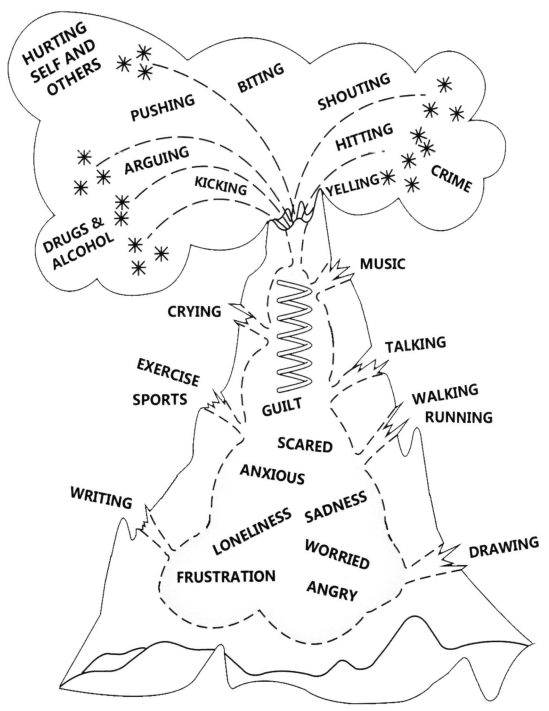

Some of the losses that may cause these feelings are: family changes, death, illness, job changes in the family, divorce, separation from loved ones, moving, developmental changes, relationship changes.

Adapted from the original with the kind permission of Ann White, MS, NCC, LMHC retired.

annsparling@gmail.com.

THOUGHTS OR FEELINGS		ACTIONS
RAGE		KILLING
HATRED		
BITTERNESS		HIT SOMEONE
ANGRY		BREAK THINGS
UNFORGIVING		SHOUT
JEALOUS		BULLY
FRUSTRATED		SAY HURTFUL THINGS
ANNOYED		CRABBY or CRITICAL
SAD OR AFRAID		SILENCE

ANGER

THOUGHTS OR FEELINGS

ACTIONS

Persian Petition for Reconciliation

All that we ought to have thought

And have not thought,

All that we ought to have said,

And have not said,

All that we ought to have done,

And have not done;

All that we ought not to have thought,

And yet have thought,

All that we ought not to have spoken,

And yet have spoken

All that we ought not to have done,

And yet have done;

For thoughts, words and works, pray we,

O God, for forgiveness.

From an ancient Persian Prayer*

*Author unknown. "**Persian Petition for Reconciliation.**" **Oxford Book of Prayer,** editor George Appleton, Published by Oxford Press Inc., New York 2009. Page number 333.

Kid Talk Lesson Plan – Week 7

Week 7: Griefwork　　　　　　　　**See Leader's Guide for Details**

Scripture & Theme	Activities (minutes) OS = *Our Story* Memory Book LG = Leader's Guide	Handouts and Take-Home Griefwork
<u>Psalm 139:16b</u> *All the days ordained for me were written in Your book before one of them came to be.* **Pray:** Lord, help me to live each day You have planned for me in a way that points others to You. Help me to trust You in the number of days that You gave to my loved one. **Theme:** What is griefwork? We have choices about what to do with our feelings.	**OPEN:** (Approximately **30** minutes) <u>Welcome:</u> Ground Rules with poster <u>Psalm 147:3:</u> ASL, discuss and pray. <u>Session Log</u>: Psalm 139:16b, discuss and pray. <u>Check-In:</u> Roll the die and name that number of feelings or behaviors of grief. **FOCUS:** (Approximately **55** minutes) (5) <u>Toilet Bowl Love</u>: OS p. 25. (Review) (20) <u>Behaviors of Grief:</u> OS p. 24. See **LG**.　<u>Griefwork:</u> OS p. 26. See **LG**.　<u>Wilted Rose:</u> review "things that would bring the rose back to life," e.g. griefwork. Include the importance of reading our Bible and talking to God. Use Grief Tips Cards. (15) <u>Marshmallow Shooter</u>: draw pictures of what you hate about having someone you love dead or gone. Pin up the pictures and shoot marshmallows at them. (15) <u>Bumper Stickers</u>: what would you like to tell the world about grieving kids on a bumper sticker? **SNACK:** (Approximately **20** minutes) Veggies and ranch dip **CLOSE:** (Approximately **15** minutes) *<u>Someday Heaven:</u>* **Read and discuss one question.** <u>Treasured Memories</u> or "Happy Snaps" <u>Session Log</u> <u>Take-Home Griefwork</u> <u>Prayer</u>	**Handouts for Adults:** Instructions for making a Marshmallow Shooter (optional) **Handouts for Kids:** • *Our Story* binders • Session Logs • Bible Verse Stickers • Half sheets for bumper stickers **Take-Home Griefwork:** • Talk about "Griefwork" and "Toilet Bowl Love" with your family. What have you done or what can you do at home? • *OS* p. 27. Talk about how your family has changed. • Discuss how you can "vent" as a family. **Next Week:** • Play **Kid Talk** version of Chutes and Ladders. • Make GAK.

NOTES

Toilet Bowl Love: *OS* p. 25. Refer to Week 6. Forgiveness is an important component of healing our grief. With God's help we can flush away hurtful words and actions as many times as necessary. God forgives and forgets. We do not forget, unfortunately. We need to flush again every time the hurt comes back.

Wilted Rose: a magic "Drooping Flower" or "Wilting Red Rose Toy" can be purchased at: www.magictricks.com. (See **Kid Talk** Supply Pantry pp 133 - 137.) It is an attention-getting way to motivate the children to name things they can do to help them through the grieving process. (Griefwork!) Say, "When someone we love dies, the life goes right out of us like this……." (Droop the flower.) "What can you do to help yourself feel better? Remember all the choices we have for doing griefwork? What are they?" Ask the children to name activities, as you slowly release the string to make the rose perk up again. Comment that it takes a lot of effort and time – more than we would like.

Marshmallow Shooter: directions for making a Mini-Marshmallow Shooter from PVC pipe can be found on the internet at www.instructables.com/id/Marshmallow-gun/. Ideally, with Covid-19 precautions in mind, have a shooter for each child and antibacterial wipes to clean them. The kids love this activity. Have them draw a picture about what they hate about grief or being a kid with a broken heart. Tape the pictures to a wall with about 10' of clearance. Important: **before shooting**, the child states what it is they hate. For example, "I hate cancer." Then he or she shoots marshmallows at the picture as a way to "vent anger." One child drew a picture of a swimming pool with a circle around it and a line through it. His baby sister drowned in their pool.

Bumper Stickers: use a half sheet of 8 ½" x 11" paper cut vertically. Invite the children to create a "bumper sticker" that tells the world what people need to know about kids' grief or about their decedent. Example: "Boys Cry Too."

Snack: veggies and ranch dip are a classic. Talk about the importance of taking good care of our bodies while we are grieving, e.g. eat healthy, get plenty of sleep and wash your hands often. Our immune system is weakened by the stress of grief, so we are more vulnerable to germs and viruses. We want to choose to practice good health habits.

- Handout for Parents/Guardians: Instructions for making a Marshmallow Shooter (optional)
- Handouts for Kids: Session Logs and Bible Verse Stickers
- Clipboard with Sign-In Sheet, pen and WELCOME sign
- Supplies to make a name place card for new arrivals
- **Our Story** binder
- Ground Rules poster
- Book: *'Someday Heaven'* and box with question cards
- Glossary Cards from www.kidtalkgrief.com/ktbaccess
- Camera for taking photos
- Hand Sanitizer

- Pencils	- Toy toilet bowl that flushes
- Pens	- Rose that wilts from a magic supply vendor
- Markers	- Basket and "Grief Tips for Kids" cards
- Box of tissues	- Mandalas and coloring sheets (bonus activity if needed)
- Basket of fiddle things (optional)	- Snack: Broccoli, carrots and celery with ranch dip
- Half sheets of paper (4 ¼" x 11") for making bumper stickers	- Small plates or bowls and napkins
- Marshmallow Shooters, a bag of mini marshmallows, antibacterial wipes and paper for drawing "targets."	- Ice water and cups

Room Set Up: A table cloth helps to identify the snack table.

Amazon Toy Flushing Toilet

Kid Talk Session Log - Week 7

Date: _____

Theme: What is griefwork? God is an important part of our healing through grief.

Series Scripture: *He heals the broken-hearted and binds up their wounds. Psalm 147:3.*

Scripture: Put scripture sticker here ➡
Psalm 139:16b

Pray:
Lord, please help me to live each
day that You have planned for me in a
way that points others to You. Help me
to trust You in the number of days that
You gave my loved one.

My <u>favorite</u> activity about this session:

☐ Scriptures   ☐ Check-In with Dice   ☐ Wilted Rose and   ☐ Behaviors of
                                                              Griefwork   Grief

☐ Marshmallow   ☐ Bumper Stickers   ☐ *Someday Heaven*   ☐ Snack- Veggies &
   Shooter   Ranch Dip

Explain your choice: _____

_____

What I want to remember from this session: _____

_____

_____

Signature   _____

Supplies Needed:

22 inches of ½" PVC pipe: cut 1 - 7" length and 5 - 3" lengths

2 end caps, 2 three-way junctions, and 2 elbows.

Assembly

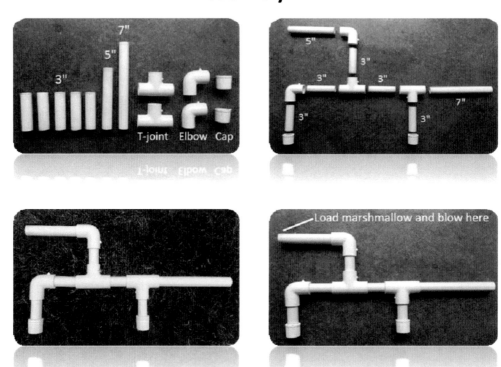

Lay out your pieces then assemble them.

Friction should hold them together.

Shooting directions:

Put on your safety glasses.

Load the mini marshmallows into the mouthpiece. Point the shooter in a safe direction. Cover the mouthpiece with your mouth and give it a quick burst of air.

The marshmallows go around all those curves.

Keep your ammunition sealed. Dry marshmallows don't work as well.

Clean up the marshmallows when you're done.

Kid Talk Lesson Plan – Week 8

Week 8: Imprints and Knowing God

See Leader's Guide for Details

Scripture & Theme	Activities (minutes) OS = *Our Story* Memory Book LG = Leader's Guide	Handouts and Take-Home Griefwork
Isaiah 26:3 NLT *You [God] will keep in perfect peace all who trust in You, all whose thoughts are fixed on You.* **Pray:** Lord, we need Your perfect peace during our grief. Help us to trust You more and focus our thoughts on You, the source of peace. **Theme:** Like a thumbprint, our decedents leave a lasting impression on our lives. Scripture helps us know God better so that we can love and trust Him more.	**OPEN:** (Approximately **30** minutes) **Welcome:** Ground Rules with poster **ASL:** Psalm 147:3, discuss and pray. **Session Log**: Isaiah 26:3 NLT, discuss and pray. **Fiddle Things:** color mandalas. **Check-In:** - Have Wilma share for the kids. Did you talk about "griefwork" with your family? Did you explain toilet bowl love? Grief vomit? **FOCUS:** (Approximately **55** minutes) **(10) Chutes and Ladders**: play the game as griefwork review. Track how many kinds of griefwork the kids can name. Offer a prize if they reach 20. See **LG**. **(20) GAK:** Children combine the ingredients to make GAK and take it home in a zip-lock baggie. Relate GAK to feelings and imprints. **(5) How My Family Has Changed**: *OS* p. 27. Complete the page with drawings of how their families have changed since the death. Talk about how hard it is to draw changes. **(10) Imprint – Your Mark on My Life:** *OS* p. 28. See **LG**. **(10) Scripture Basket**: Let each child choose a scripture card from the basket to read out loud and tell how it can help them. This is griefwork. **SNACK:** (Approximately **20** minutes) Sea Turtles **CLOSE:** (Approximately **15** minutes) *Someday Heaven*: **Read and discuss one question.** **Session Log** **Take-Home Griefwork** **Happy Snaps** **Prayer**	**Handouts for Adults:** Scripture Verses for the Bereaved **Handouts for Kids:** • *Our Story* binders • Session Logs • Bible Verse Stickers • GAK recipe **Take-Home Griefwork:** • **Discuss OS** p. 28 with your family. Have they been imprinted differently than you? • Share this week's scripture with your family and pray together. **Next Week:** • Make Dream Catchers. • Dip Pretzel Sticks.

NOTES

Chutes and Ladders: Kid Talk Chutes and Ladders is played as a review of grief triggers and griefwork. Extra game markers can be purchased on Amazon for about $5. After spinning to determine how many squares to advance, the child names something he has done, could do, or will do to help himself move forward in healing his own grief. If they fall down a chute, they tell what can keep us from healing or interfere with our own healing process. Record griefwork choices on p. 26 of *OS*.

Imprints – Your Mark on My Life: *Our Story* p. 28. Talk about imprints, what they are and how we can choose to view them as part of our griefwork. Let the conversation flow into making GAK or while waiting a few minutes for the GAK to "season."

GAK (or "Slime"): can be made in individual portions using 4-ounce bottles of white glue. It can also be made as a cooperative project using a larger bottle of glue. The recipe is with this lesson. Children take home their GAK in a zip lock baggie. Ask the children to explain how GAK resembles grief: it doesn't stay the same, it isn't predictable, it might not feel or look good and people might shy away from it. Ask, "Does GAK accept imprints? What imprints did your decedent make on your life?" Record them on p. 28 of *Our Story*.

How My Family Has Changed: *OS* p. 27. Ask the children to complete the pages with drawings of how their families have changed since the death. Talk about how their lives are different now. How are the people in their family different because they are grieving? What changes are hard to see? How will their families look a year from now?

Scripture Basket: a list of printable scripture cards for each session is with this lesson or at www.kidtalkgrief.com/ktbaccess. These can be printed, cut apart and laminated. Put them in a basket and invite the children to choose one and discuss it. How can Scripture help our grief? It reminds us of God's love and care for us. It reminds us of God's promises to us. It gives us hope. Scripture is how we get to know God better. The better we know Him, the easier it is to trust Him and His love for us. Reading Scripture and talking to God, e.g. praying, are important choices we can make that help us heal.

Apple Sea Turtles: supplies needed include green apples, grapes, mini chocolate chips, goldfish crackers for garnish, and a paper plate for display. Apple turtles are made by cutting a green apple in half and putting it on a plate. Slice grapes in half and arrange them as flippers. Slice off one third of a grape for the head. Using the point of a knife, puncture two small holes in the grape, one for each eye. Press mini chocolate chips, pointy side down into the holes. Ask the children if they can think of reasons that turtles might be like grief. Turtles are slow and very vulnerable when young. Kids will take years to work through their losses AND will most likely re-work or recycle their grief in their teen years. Expect it to happen. Turtles can float and relax in the underwater current. We can "float" in God's loving arms, knowing that He loves us and will direct our steps towards a good life if we choose to get to know Him better and better.

- Handouts for Parents/Guardians: Scripture Verses for the Bereaved
- Handouts for Kids: Session Logs and Bible Verse Stickers, GAK Recipe
- Clipboard with Sign-In Sheet, pen, and WELCOME sign
- Supplies to make a name place card for new arrivals
- *Our Story* binder
- Ground Rules poster
- Book: *'Someday Heaven'* and box with question cards
- Glossary Cards from www.kidtalkgrief.com/ktbaccess
- Camera for taking photos of the kids making GAK
- Hand Sanitizer

- Pens and pencils
- Markers
- Box of tissues
- Basket of fiddle things (optional)
- Game: Chutes and Ladders with enough place markers
- Supplies for making GAK: electric tea pot for hot water, measuring cups, mixing spoons, small mixing bowls or containers, food coloring, 1-qt. zip lock baggies to take GAK home.
  Directions: Pour 4 oz. of white glue into a small container with ½ cup of water. Mix with a spoon, then stir in a few drops of food coloring. In a separate container, dissolve ½ teaspoon of borax into ¼ cup of warm water. Stir until it is completely dissolved, or it will fail. Pour dissolved borax into the glue mix and stir. Now you have "Rubber Blubber" or GAK.

- Scriptures on laminated cards in a small basket
- Basket of Grief Tips for Kids cards
- Mandalas and coloring sheets (bonus activity if needed)
- Snack: Apple Sea Turtles are made using green apples, green grapes, miniature chocolate chips and goldfish crackers on paper plates.
- Cups, napkins, and ice water

Room Set Up: a tablecloth helps to identify the snack table.

Kid Talk Session Log – Week 8

Date: _____

Theme: 1. Like a thumbprint, our decedents leave a lasting impression on our lives. 2. Reading our Bibles and talking to God every day is an important part of our peace and healing.

Series Scripture: *He heals the broken-hearted and binds up their wounds. Psalm 147:3.*

Scripture: Put scripture sticker here ➡
Isaiah 26:3 NLT

Pray:
Lord, we need Your perfect peace during our grief. Help us to trust You more and focus our thoughts on You, the source of peace.

My <u>favorite</u> activity about this session:

☐ Check-In with Wilma   ☐ Chutes and Ladders   ☐ Imprints   ☐ How My Family has Changed

☐ GAK   ☐ Scripture Basket   ☐ *Someday Heaven*   ☐ Snack – Sea Turtles

Explain your choice: _____

_____

What I want to remember from this session: _____

_____

_____

Signature _____

GAK

Use **two** separate containers.

In the first container mix together:

2 cups Elmer's Glue

2 cups water

5-10 drops of food coloring

In the second container stir until **completely** dissolved:

1 cup **warm** water

2 Tbs Borax

Pour dissolved Borax mix into glue mix.

As soon as the borax hits the glue mix it hardens!

Mix it with your hands until it is smooth.

Put it on a plate.

Leave it 15 minutes to flatten.

Store in an AIRTIGHT container.

1 I cry to You for help when my heart is overwhelmed. Lead me to the towering rock of safety. PSALM 61:2b NLT	**2** He has sent me [Jesus] ... to comfort all who mourn. ISAIAH 61:1b-2
3 God is our refuge and strength, an ever-present help in trouble. PSALM 46:1	**4** I wait for the LORD, my whole being waits, and in His word I put my hope. PSALM 130:5
5 The LORD is close to the broken-hearted and saves those who are crushed in spirit. PSALM 34:18	**6** The secret things belong to the LORD our God. DEUTERONOMY 29:29a
7 All the days ordained for me were written in Your book before one of them came to be. PSALM 139:16b	**8** You [God] will keep in perfect peace all who trust in You, all whose thoughts are fixed on You! ISAIAH 26:3 NLT

9 Trust in the Lord with all your heart: do not depend on your own understanding. PROVERBS 3:5 NLT	**10** For I can do everything through Christ, who gives me strength. PHILIPPIANS 4:13 NLT
11 But God demonstrates His own love for us in this: While we were still sinners, Christ died for us. ROMANS 5:8	**12** He will wipe every tear from their eyes. There will be no more death or mourning or crying or pain, for the old order of things has passed away. REVELATION 21:4
13 But those who hope in the LORD will renew their strength. They will soar on wings like eagles: they will run and not grow weary, they will walk and not be faint. ISAIAH 40:31	**O** He heals the broken hearted and binds up their wounds. PSALMS 147:3 TRUTH: God is healing my broken heart.
For [God] will turn their mourning into joy and will comfort them and give them joy for their sorrow. JEREMIAH 31:13 NAS	Draw near to God and He will draw near to you. JAMES 4:8a

Scripture Verses for the Bereaved

The following are the scriptures that we use at Kid Talk:

Orientation - Psalm 147:3
He heals the brokenhearted and binds up their wounds.

Week 1 - Psalm 61:2b NLT
I cry to you for help when my heart is overwhelmed. Lead me to the towering rock of safety.

Week 2 - Isaiah 61:1b-2
He has sent me [Jesus]….to comfort all who mourn.

Week 3 - Psalm 46:1
God is our refuge and strength, an ever present help in trouble.

Week 4 – Psalm 130:5
I wait for the LORD, my whole being waits, and in His Word I put my hope.

Week 5 - Psalm 34:18
The LORD is close to the broken-hearted and saves those who are crushed in spirit.

Week 6 - Deuteronomy 29:29a
The secret things belong to the Lord our God.

Week 7 - Psalm 139:16b
All the days ordained for me were written in your book before one of them came to be.

Week 8 - Isaiah 26:3 NLT
You [God] will keep in perfect peace all who trust in you, all whose thoughts are fixed on you.

Week 9 - Proverbs 3:5 NLT
Trust in the Lord with all your heart; do not depend on your own understanding.

Week 10 - Philippians 4:13 NLT
For I can do everything through Christ, who gives me strength.

Week 11 - Romans 5:8
But God demonstrates His own love for us in this: While we were still sinners, Christ died for us.

Week 12 - Rev. 21:4
He will wipe every tear from their eyes. There will be no more death or mourning or crying or pain, for the old order of things has passed away.

Week 13 - Isaiah 40:31
But those who hope in the Lord will renew their strength. They will soar on wings like eagles: they will run and not grow weary; they will walk and not be faint.

We also like these scriptures: (They are in our basket of scripture verses.)

Jeremiah 31:13
For [God] will turn their mourning into joy and will comfort them and give them joy for their sorrow.

Isaiah 53: 4a
Surely He has borne our griefs and carried our sorrows;

James 4: 8a
Draw near to God and He will draw near to you.

John 16:22
Therefore you now have sorrow; but I will see you again and your heart will rejoice, and your joy no one will take from you.

Kid Talk Lesson Plan – Week 9

Week 9: Dreams and Feeling Safe   See Leader's Guide for Details

Scripture & Theme	Activities (minutes) OS = *Our Story* Memory Book LG = Leader's Guide	Handouts and Take-Home Griefwork

Proverbs 3:5 NLT
Trust in the Lord with all your heart; do not depend on your own understanding.
 	
Pray:
Lord, we don't understand everything about death and grief. Please help us to trust You with our whole heart anyway, even though we are hurting.
 	
Theme:
We can talk to our dreams because we write them.
 	
God is always with us.
	OPEN: (Approximately **30** minutes)
	Welcome: Ground Rules with poster
	ASL: Psalm 147:3, discuss and pray.
	Session Log: Proverbs 3:5 NLT, discuss and pray.
	Check-In: roll a multi-colored die. Have Wilma, the Pop-Up puppet, talk about the topic that matches the color on the top side of the die.
	    Red = feelings of grief
	    Blue = griefwork
	    Yellow = grief behaviors
	
	FOCUS: (Approximately **55** minutes)
	(10) Dreams: *OS* p. 29. Have you dreamt about your decedent? How did you feel when you woke up? What are choices that we can make about dealing with our dreams?
	(30) Make Dream Catchers: Choose dream catchers suitable to the skill level of your group. There is a large variety. See **LG.**
	(10) My Circle of Support: **OS** p. 30. Who "is there" for you to talk to? Not all kids have a good circle of support. How can we help them?
	(5) My Safe Place: **OS** p. 31. Why do we need a safe place? Can everyone have one? When do you go there?
	
	SNACK: (Approximately **20** minutes)
	Apple Sandwiches
	
	CLOSE: (Approximately **15** minutes)
	Someday Heaven: **choose, read and discuss one question.**
	Happy Snaps
	Session Log
	Take-Home Griefwork: *OS* p. 33.
	Prayer
		Handouts for Adults:
		"Understanding Nightmares" by Bob Baugher, Ph.D.
		
		Handouts for Kids:
		• *Our Story* binders
		• Session Logs
		• Bible Verse Stickers
		• How to Weave a Dream Catcher
		• Butterfly Coloring Page
		
		Take Home Griefwork:
		OS p. 33. Think of seven special memories for your "Bouquet of Memories."
		
		Next Week:
		We will make a bouquet of tissue paper flowers.

NOTES

Colored Dice: a set of 6 colored-dice can be ordered from Amazon. These have a different color on each side: red, orange, yellow, green, blue, purple. Let the kids determine the color coding, then take turns rolling the die and sharing on that topic. Make one color a "pass." Another option is a 4" die (Amazon) that has whiteboard sides on which you can write "PASS" on one side and "Talk Topics" on the other five sides. They might be: Griefwork, Feelings, Grief Bundle, Safe Place, Dreams. Include review topics or issues you want to revisit with conversation.

Dreams: *OS* p. 29. Our dreams come from our own subconscious. Say, "Did you know that we write our own dreams. In the Bible God spoke to people in their dreams: Abraham and Joseph in the Old Testament and Mary, Peter, and John in the New Testament. There are others too. God has also given us authority over everything (Matthew 16:19), so we can speak to our dreams and tell them to go away. We can ask God to help us re-write our dreams with a happy ending. We can also ask God for angels to watch over us. (Psalm 91:11)"

Dream Catchers: Explain that, "Native American moms have placed "Dream Catchers" above their sleeping babies in the belief the bad dreams would be caught in the web and perish with the light of dawn. The good dreams would pass through the little hole in the middle to the sleeping baby. There are a lot of dream catchers for sale in the southwest part of the United States. They can be simple and lovely or very complex and expensive. They are beautiful and fun to make, so we will."

www.artbarblog.com/diy-dream-catchers-made-by-kids

or www.dream-catchers.org/make-a-dream-catcher-for-kids

or www.instructables.com/id/How-to-make-a-Dreamcatcher-2

To make a simple dream catcher visit:
These are examples of different levels of difficulty. Using paper plates, yarn, plastic pony beads and craft feathers, works for the younger children. The rims of plastic lids and embroidery floss are nice also. The web wrapping is simple once you catch on. See the printed diagram and practice!

My Circle of Support: *OS* p. 30. Consider sharing the following: God loves us and made us in His image. He is our number one support. God created us to be in fellowship with Him, with our families and with our friends and neighbors. He made us to need Him and to need each other. We all need "A Circle of Support." Jesus had the disciples.

We have **Kid Talk** with new friends who understand what it's like to be a kid with a broken heart. God loves to hear from us in conversation or prayer. God provides parents to love and take care of us when we are young. He provides other adults for kids, too, who care and listen and have wisdom and experience to guide you. Ask, "Who has He provided for you? A relative? A teacher or counselor? A church leader or pastor? Let us Pray for children who may not have the circle of support that we do."

My Safe Place: *OS* p. 31. Jesus withdrew from his disciples to be alone and pray. We also need time alone where it is safe. Ask, "Where is your safe place? Mine is in my big chair with a comforter. Is it in your room? Your back yard? At your grandma's house? Did you build it yourself? Draw a picture of your safe place."

- Handouts for Parents/Guardians: "Understanding Nightmares" by Bob Baugher, Ph.D.
- Handouts for Kids: Session Logs and Bible Verse Stickers, How to Weave a Dream Catcher
- Clipboard with Sign-In Sheet, pen and WELCOME sign
- Supplies needed to make a name place card for new arrivals
- ***Our Story*** binder
- Ground Rules poster
- Book: '*Someday Heaven*' and box with question cards
- Wilma, Pop-Up Puppet
- Glossary Cards from www.kidtalkgrief.com/ktbaccess
- Camera for taking photos
- Hand Sanitizer

- Pencils
- Pens
- Markers
- Box of tissues
- Colored die
- Basket of fiddle things (optional)
- Dream Catcher Supplies: paper plates, scissors, hole punch, 3' to 4' lengths of colored yarn, tape, plastic beads, craft feathers, and the handout "How to Weave a Dream Catcher." (p. 100)

- Mandalas and coloring sheets
- Snack: Apple sandwiches. One Granny Smith apple makes 5 apple sandwiches. You will need 10 Tbs peanut butter, 1 Granny Smith apple cored and cut into 10 rings, each about ¼ inch thick, 5 Tbs. granola, and 2 Tbs. raisins. Spread 2 Tbs. peanut butter onto half of the apple rings. Sprinkle each with 1 Tbs. granola and a few raisins. Cover each with one of the remaining apple rings to form sandwiches.
- Paper plates, knives, napkins
- Cups and ice water

Room Set Up: A tablecloth helps to identify the snack table.

Date: _____

Theme: 1. We can talk to our dreams because we write them! 2. We can always talk to God and trust Him to be with us no matter what.

Series Scripture: *God will heal my broken heart. Psalm 147:3.*

Scripture: Put scripture sticker here ➡
Proverbs 3:5 NLT

Pray:
Lord, we don't understand everything about death and grief. Please help us to trust You with our whole heart anyway, even though we are hurting.
Thank You for Kid Talk.

My <u>favorite</u> activity about this session:

☐ Check-In with   ☐ Being with Other   ☐ Dreams and   ☐ My Circle of
   Colored Dice   Grieving Kids   Dream Catchers   Support

☐ My Safe Place   ☐ Happy Snaps   ☐ *Someday Heaven*   ☐ Snack – Apple
                                              Sandwiches

Explain your choice: _____

_____

What I want to remember from this session: _____

_____

_____

Signature _____

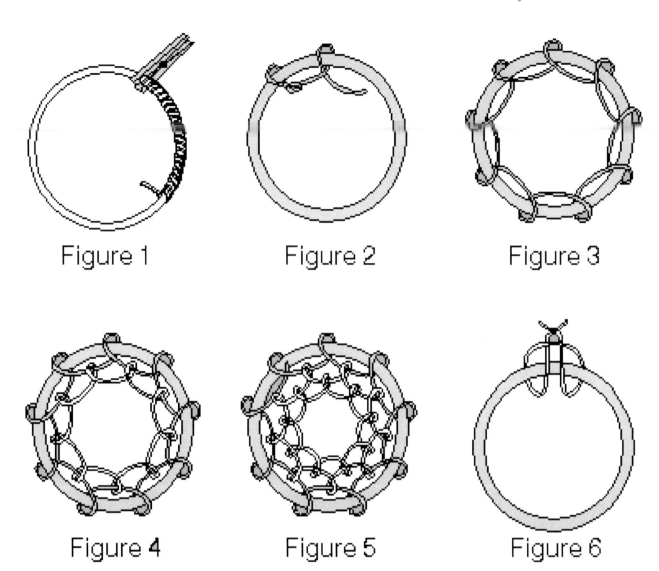

Figure 1   Figure 2   Figure 3

Figure 4   Figure 5   Figure 6

For instructions visit:

www.muminthemadhouse.com/diy-dreamcatcher-tutorial **OR** www.tinyfry.com/make-dream-catcher-kids

Understanding Nightmares

Bob Baugher, Ph.D.

This is a follow-up article to the topic of dreams. Let's look at the negative side of dreams. Nightmares, especially those concerning your child, can be very disturbing. Let's look at some facts and suggestions.

1. The average person has 1-2 nightmares per year. However, people who have experienced trauma in their life (such as death) may have more nightmares because the brain is attempting to gradually incorporate the information into the memory.

2. Most researchers categorize "bad dreams" as either *REM* (rapid eye movement) *Anxiety Dreams* or *Night Terrors*.

3. *REM Anxiety Dreams* consist of detailed anxiety-producing content. The dreamer awakens remembering an upsetting story of a set of events. You may have dreamed about the death of your child all over again, or your dream may have involved you rediscovering the horrible fact of your child's death. Perhaps you dreamed your child, you, or some third party behaved in a negative manner. As I stated in my previous article on dreams, if you dream something negative, it does not mean that this is what you *really wanted*. Your brain can create all kinds of bizarre, unsettling, and incomprehensible stories—all for senseless reasons. Remember, when you sleep, your brain is bathed in chemicals that help to create stories that defy logic. And if anyone can interpret a dream, it is you by asking yourself the question: *What is my brain trying to tell me?* And if no answer comes, then chalk it up to your brain going on its own incomprehensible tangent. Don't let anyone else try to interpret your dream for you. The rule is: *If the dreamer can't figure it out, no one can.*

4. *Night Terrors* most often occur within a couple hours after falling asleep and take place in Stage 4 (the deepest level of sleep). The dreamer remembers little, if any, detail. If something is remembered, it is typically a single frightening event, such as "I was choking," or "There was something heavy on my chest." A scream may precede the awakening and the person is disoriented for several minutes afterward. Most experts consider *Night Terrors* to be a physically caused problem in which, for unknown reasons, the person's autonomic nervous (fight or flight) system becomes activated.

5. Starting or stopping medications as well as alcohol use can cause an increase in a person's nightmare frequency. This fact further supports the contention that dreams are stimulated by random chemical reactions to the brain.

6. Here are two suggestions for coping with a nightmare:

- Talk about it. Find a caring person who will let you "get it off your chest." Keeping it inside gives the nightmare more power. Gain control of it by talking it out.
- Write out the dream as you remember it. Then turn over the paper and rewrite the story the way you'd *like* it to be. Just before going to sleep sit on your bed and rehearse it a few times. Continue this for a few days and the dream should begin to change.
- To repeat: no matter how frightening or disturbing the dream, it is important that you get it "outside of your head" by talking it out or writing it down.

For example, let's say that you dreamed your son or daughter said something terrible to you. First, tell someone. Next, write out every detail and then create a new version. In this example, you might write that the dream ends with your child suddenly smiling and saying, "Just kidding, Mom (or Dad). You know I love you and miss you and from where I am now, I feel nothing but love." You might complete the story by saying, "Then we hugged for the longest time and it felt wonderful."

7. If you have other children who have had nightmares, especially about their deceased brother or sister, the following advice may help:

Upon entering the room of a child who has just had a nightmare, turn on a lamp rather than an overhead light. The more light our eyes take in upon awakening, the more difficult it is to return to sleep. As you approach your child try to get him or her back to sleep. If this doesn't work, hold your child and encourage the telling of the nightmare. Listen without interruption, encouraging the story to be told from start to finish. As the child shares the dream, acknowledge how frightening it must have been and assure your child that he or she is safe. Do this several times during the dream-telling. Review the dream the next morning using the same technique whether or not your child told you the dream the night before. Most parents find it helpful to allow the child to keep on a night light for a few days or weeks following a nightmare episode.

The grief reactions you or your family members are experiencing may sometimes come out in the form of dreams or nightmares. By following these suggestions, you should be able to take some control of this process. If this doesn't work and your life continues to be disrupted from these night disturbances, you may want to get some help from a counselor or therapist.

And now that you are at the end of this article, I bet you knew I was going to say:
I wish you only sweet dreams.

See Dr. Bob's entire article on dreams at www.bobbaugher.com

Dr. Bob Baugher, Highline Community College, Des Moines, Washington.

Week 10: Memories   See Leader's Guide for Details

Scripture & Theme	Activities (minutes) *OS* = *Our Story* Memory Book **LG** = **Leader's Guide**	Handouts and Take-Home Griefwork
Phil. 4:13 NLT *For I can do everything through Christ, who gives me strength.* **Pray:** Lord, please help each of us to do well in school. Give us Your strength to be kind and loving like You. **Theme:** Memories are an important part of healing. One of the ways that God gives us strength is through the support of people who care about us.	**OPEN:** (Approximately **30** minutes) **Welcome:** Ground Rules with poster **ASL:** Psalm 147:3, discuss and pray. **Session Log: Phil. 4:13 NLT**, discuss and pray. **Check-In:** play rock, paper, scissors. Winner shares about their safe place, their circle of support or a treasured memory. The winner may also choose someone else to share. **FOCUS:** (Approximately **55** minutes) **(10) Will I Heal?** *OS* p.32. Discuss what healing means and does not mean. We have the hope of healing from our broken hearts. How will we look then? **(10) Bouquet of Memories:** *OS* p.33. Discuss revisiting memories to do griefwork. Could you make a bouquet of gratitude? **(30) Tissue Paper Flowers and Butterflies:** What memory does each of the seven flowers represent? How can flowers and butterflies help us do griefwork? **(5) Butterfly Craft or Coloring Pages:** (If there is time.) See **LG**. **SNACK:** (Approximately **20** minutes) **Flowerpot Pudding Cups:** our floral snack also reminds us that we have a bouquet of memories. Or **Butterfly Snack Bags** with trail mix. **CLOSE:** (Approximately **15** minutes) *Someday Heaven*: **choose, read and discuss one question.** **Session Log** **Take-Home Grief Work** **Happy Snaps** **Prayer**	**Handouts for Adults:** *"Helping A Grandparent Who is Grieving"* by Alan D. Wolfelt, Ph.D. **Handouts for Kids:** • *Our Story* binders • Session Logs • Bible Verse Stickers • Butterfly coloring pages **Take-Home Griefwork:** • Share with your family the memories that your bouquet recalls for you. Learn their memories. • Cut out pictures and words from magazines that remind you of your decedent. **Next Week:** We will decoupage cigar boxes to make memory boxes.

NOTES

Will I Heal? *OS* p. 32 presents the opportunity to review what it means for our grief to "heal." It is important to talk about what it does not mean. Basically, we want to remember our decedent without emotional pain and have the energy to invest in normal living. It does not mean that we will never have grief pains again. Kids **will** re-grieve because their grief will "recycle" as they mature. That's why it is so great to have an *Our Story* **Memory Book** to help them revisit grief close to the time it happened. Doing so can be helpful griefwork.

Bouquet of Memories: *OS* p. 33 is another way of doing griefwork by revisiting memories. We share a lot of memories at **Kid Talk**. This is a variation of "Happy Snaps." Kids often share they are afraid that they will forget. There are seven flowers in the bouquet on p. 33. Hopefully, there will be time for each child to make seven tissue paper flowers. Because the memories are written down, the child will be able to remember them again someday – or at least re-connect with the memory from when they were younger. Explain that, "When you are five, ten or twenty years older than you are now, it will help you do griefwork to look at what you've put in your Bouquet of Memories today."

Tissue Paper Flowers: the internet has multiple patterns and demonstrations for making tissue paper flowers. (For example, www.creativelive.com/blog/how-to-make-a-tissue-paper-flower.) Choose flowers within the skill sets of your group. Each of the flowers represents a memory. The kids like it when a vase or jar is provided to put their bouquets in, to take home. The child can share his or her own memories and ask family members for their top seven.

Butterfly Craft: there are multiple ways to make butterflies requiring different amounts of time and supplies. A favorite is using two round coffee filters, clothes pins, googly eyes and half a pipe cleaner. Color the coffee filter with markers or drops of diluted food coloring.

> **See**: www.yourmodernfamily.com/butterfly-crafts-with-coffee-filters, www.happyhooligans.ca/butterfly-crafts-for-kids or www.redtedart.com/rainbow-butterfly-cork-crafts

Flower Pot Pudding Cups: here is one of many recipes for these kid-pleasing treats: www.thetiptoefairy.com/flower-pot-pudding-cups.

Butterfly Snack Bags: here is one of many recipes for these fun treats with potentially less sugar content: www.momeefriendsli.com.

- Handouts for Parents/Guardians: "Helping a Grandparent Who is Grieving" by Alan D. Wolfelt, Ph.D.
- Handouts for Kids: Session Log and Bible Verse Stickers, Butterfly Coloring Page
- Clipboard with Sign-In Sheet, pen, and WELCOME sign
- Supplies to make a name place card for new arrivals
- *Our Story* binder
- Ground Rules poster
- Book: '*Someday Heaven*' and box with question cards
- Glossary Cards from www.kidtalkgrief.com/ktbaccess
- Camera for taking photos of the kids
- Hand Sanitizer

- Pens and pencils
- Markers
- Box of tissues
- Basket of fiddle things (optional)
- Tissue Paper Flowers require scissors, different colored sheets of tissue paper, printed directions or diagrams, pipe cleaners or floral wires, straws, vases or jars. Prepare a sample bouquet so the kids can see what they will make.
- Butterfly Craft – It is unlikely there will be time to make butterflies. The Leader's Guide offers suggestions that are good to have on hand for a future session. The Butterfly Snack Bags are also a craft.

- Flowerpot Pudding Cups can be found at www.thetiptoefairy.com/flower-pot-pudding-cups Supplies needed include Super Snack Pudding Packs in chocolate, small lollipops, green sprinkles, marshmallows, and Oreos.
- Alternately, make Butterfly Snack Bags. See: www.bing.com/search?q=butterfly+snack+bags&form=EDGHPT&qs=PF&cvid=2482a0fbb69846b7a53702f9c84f70d9&refig=6fca4b80fb104120869ff9047905ff03&cc=US&setlang=en-US&plvar=0&PC=MSE1 Besides edible snack food for filler, you will need paints, clothespins, sandwich bags, pipe cleaners, googly eyes and a hot glue gun.
- Ice water, cups, plates, and napkins

Room Set Up: a tablecloth helps to identify the snack table.

Kid Talk Session Log – Week 10

Date: _____

Theme: 1. Memories are griefwork. 2. One of the ways that God gives us strength is through the support of people who care about us.

Series Scripture: *He heals the broken-hearted and binds up their wounds. Psalm 147:3.*

Scripture: Put scripture sticker here ➡
Philippians 4:13 NLT.

Pray:
Lord, thank You for giving us Your strength when we need it. Please help each of us to do the next thing. Give us Your strength so that we can be kind and loving like You.

My <u>favorite</u> activity about this session:

☐ Scriptures ☐ Check-In with Rock, Paper, Scissors. ☐ Will I Heal? ☐ Bouquet of Memories

☐ Tissue Paper Flowers ☐ Butterfly Craft ☐ *Someday Heaven* ☐ Snack – Flower Pot Pudding Cups

Explain your choice: _____

What I want to remember from this session: _____

_____

_____

_____
Signature

Kid Talk Lesson Plan – Week 11

Week 11: Gratitude   See Leader's Guide for Details

Scripture & Theme	Activities (minutes) *OS* = *Our Story* Memory Book LG = Leader's Guide	Handouts and Take-Home Griefwork
Romans 5:8 *But God demonstrates His own love for us in this: While we were still sinners, Christ died for us.* **Pray:** Dear Lord, thank You for loving me so much that You died for me. Thank You that I can look forward to being in heaven with my loved ones because I accept Your sacrifice for me. **Theme:** Gratitude helps us get through grief.	**OPEN:** (Approximately **30** minutes) **Welcome:** Ground Rules with poster **Psalm 147: 3** ASL, discuss and pray. **Session Log: Romans 5:8**, discuss and pray. **Check-In:** use Wilma, to share: What grief work did you share with your family this last week? What *is* gratitude? For what are you grateful? **FOCUS:** (Approximately **55** minutes) **(10) My Gratitude List:** *OS* p. 34. It is a healthy habit to "count our blessings" at the beginning of the day. Gratitude is an attitude. **(10) Treasured Memories:** *OS* p. 35. Record treasured memories on the printed coins and cut them out. Insert them into the treasure chest. Discuss memories as griefwork. Discuss the value of a "Memory Box." See **LG** p. 109. **(25) Make a Memory Box:** decoupage magazine pictures and words that are reminders of the person who died, onto a cigar box. While working, talk about what can be put in the memory/treasure box, both now and in the future. (e.g. - Valentines, Father's Day or Mother's Day cards, memorabilia, etc.) **SNACK:** (Approximately **20** minutes) **Banana Palm Trees:** (See **LG**) Palm trees withstand storms and hurricanes. They bend but do not break. Us too. We will get back to being ourselves. See **LG**. **CLOSE:** (Approximately **15** minutes) *Someday Heaven:* **Read and discuss one question.** **Session Log** **Take-Home Griefwork: Special Letter, *OS* p. 37.** **Happy Snaps** **Prayer**	**Handouts for Adults:** Online Resources **Handouts for Kids:** • *Our Story* binders • Session Logs • Bible Verse Stickers • Page of Gold Coins **Take-Home Griefwork:** *OS* p. 37 - Write a "Special Letter" **Next Week:** • Make a doily envelope for our letters. • Do an exercise with shoes. • Play **Kid Talk** Jenga.

NOTES

"Wilma," the Pop-Up Puppet has been previously introduced. The children will have the opportunity to make a puppet of their own in Week 13 (p. 125). Using her this session will increase their enthusiasm for making their own puppet.

My Gratitude List: *OS* p. 34 is an important lesson in the power of gratitude towards our good mental health and the healing of our grief. The Bible says we are to be thankful **IN** all things. That is not **FOR** them, but in the midst of them. We trust God when we don't understand. His thoughts are higher than our thoughts. (He is smarter!) He has asked us to be thankful. It is for our own well-being. Let's take time to "count our blessings." It is really a good habit to do this every morning or at some point every day.

Treasured Memories: *OS* p. 35. Photocopy coins on gold paper or print a PDF of gold coins from www.kidtalkgrief.com/ktbaccess. Give each child a half-sheet to cut out. Prepare the pages before the children arrive as follows: use an X-acto knife to make a horizontal slit across the top of the treasure chest. Use a glue stick around all the open edges of a 3"x 6 ½" envelope and place it on the back of the page over the opening in the treasure chest. The children can then insert the coins with their treasured memories into the chest. Challenge the children to remember things that were not in their floral bouquet of memories. They may take extra coins home and invite their families to add memories.

Treasured Memory Boxes: are an all time favorite of the kids. Obtain cigar boxes from a local smoke shop. They will often donate them for your purpose. Each child decoupages magazine pictures and words that remind them of their person who died onto the outside and/or inside of their box with Mod Podge. Be careful not to let glue get on the top edges of the box so the lid sticks closed. Figure out a way to prop them open until they dry. Ask the children if they have something that belonged to their person who died. Will it fit into their memory box? What might they like to add in the future? Seasonal cards? Photos? The memory box gives us a place to keep "connecting links" with our decedent.

Banana Palm Tree: www.mommysfabulousfinds.com/fruit-palm-tree-how-to-get-kids-to-eat-fruit. These are made by splitting a banana in half lengthwise and laying the flat sides down curved away from each other on a plate. Cut Kiwi slices in half to make the palm branches with sections of fresh mandarin oranges at the base. Palm trees can withstand heavy storms: so can we, with God's help.

- Handouts for Parents/Guardians: Online Resources
- Handouts for Kids: Session Log and Bible Verse Stickers, Page of Gold Coins
- Clipboard with Sign-In Sheet, pen and WELCOME sign
- Name place cards and supplies to make one for new attendees
- ***Our Story*** binder
- Ground Rules poster
- Book: '*Someday Heaven*' and box with question cards
- Glossary Cards from www.kidtalkgrief.com/ktbaccess
- Camera for taking photos of the kids

- Pencils - Pens - Markers - Box of tissues - Wilma, the Pop-Up-Puppet - Basket of fiddle things (optional) - Supplies for making Memory Boxes: cigar boxes, lots of magazine words - and pictures, scissors, Mod Podge, - sponge brushes (White glue mixed - with equal parts of water works also.)	- Snack: Banana Palm Trees (See Leader's Guide) Bananas, Kiwi Fruit, Mandarin oranges - Plates, napkins, plastic knives - Paper cups and ice water - Hand sanitizer

Room Set Up: a table cloth helps to identify the snack table.

Wilma & Friends

Kid Talk Session Log – Week 11

Date: _____

Theme: Gratitude helps us through grief. What can we be grateful for? Our salvation and our memories!

Series Scripture: *He heals the broken-hearted and binds up their wounds. Psalm 147:3.*

Scripture: Put scripture sticker here ➡
Romans 5:8

Pray:
Dear Lord, thank You for loving me so much that You died for me. Thank You that I can look forward to being in heaven with my loved ones because I accept Your sacrifice for me.

My <u>favorite</u> activity about this session:

☐ Scriptures   ☐ Check-In   ☐ Gratitude List   ☐ Treasured Memories
                          with Wilma

☐ Make a Memory   ☐ *Someday*   ☐ Happy Snaps   ☐ Snack – Banana Palm
Box   *Heaven*   Tree

Explain your choice: _____

_____

What I want to remember from this session: _____

_____

_____

Signature _____

Online Resources

American Foundation of Suicide Prevention whose mission it is to save lives and support those impacted by suicide. www.afsp.org.

Bob Baugher, Ph.D. is a psychologist, college instructor, certified death educator, author, and speaker. He covers a large spectrum of topics in his books, articles, and videos. www.bobbaugher.com

Center for Loss and Life Transition – Organization dedicated to helping people who are grieving and those who care for them. Dr. Alan D. Wolfelt, Ph.D.

ChildrenGrieve.org/resources – National Alliance for Grieving Children/Resources

CounselingWithHeart.com – 6 Ways to Help Children Process the Death of a Pet

Ctainc.com - Remembering My Someone Special Grieving Journal for Kids (24 pp.) $0.99.

GriefCounselor.org/resources/helpful-websites/ - Center for Grief Recovery and Therapeutic Services

GriefNet.org – an internet community of people with resources

GriefShare.org – a network of grief recovery support groups around the world created and supported by Church Initiative.

OpenToHope.com – Articles, videos, and podcasts about coping with specific types of losses with Dr. Gloria Horsley

National Alliance for Grieving Children/resources - has a list of helpful websites.

Pinterest.com – search for "kid's grief activities."

SuperColoring.com. – free coloring pages of all kinds

Survivors of Suicide – grief support for survivors of suicide

TeachersPayTeachers.com/search/children's grief

The Compassionate Friends – support families who have had a child die, www.compassionatefriends.org

The National Center for Grieving Children and Families - TheDougyCenter.org
- *Children, Teens, and Suicide Loss* booklet
- *After A Murder*

UnityHospice.org/grief-support

Kid Talk Lesson Plan– Week 12

Week 12: Memorializing   **See Leader's Guide for Details**

Scripture & Theme	Activities (minutes) OS = *Our Story* Memory Book LG = Leader's Guide	Handouts and Take-Home Griefwork
<u>Rev. 21:4</u> *He will wipe every tear from their eyes. There will be no more death or mourning or crying or pain, for the old order of things has passed away.* **Pray:** Dear Lord, thank You that we can look forward to being in heaven forever. Thank You that we will never have a broken heart again when we are there with You. **Theme:** Memorializing: we can still show our love for the person who died. Heaven is our destiny.	**OPEN:** (Approximately **30** minutes) <u>Welcome:</u> Ground Rules with poster <u>Psalm 147:3</u>: ASL, discuss and pray. <u>Session Log:</u> Rev. 21:4, discuss and pray. <u>Check-In:</u> what are ways that we can continue to show our love for someone who is no longer here? – Memorialize. **FOCUS:** (Approximately **55** minutes) **(10)** <u>Shoes:</u> choose a pair of shoes (picture) that reminds you of your decedent and stand on it. Why did you choose that pair? What would you like to say to him or her? What would he or she say back to you? **(10)** <u>Love You Forever:</u> *OS* p. 36. We can make our love visible even though our decedents aren't here. **(15)** <u>A Special Letter:</u> *OS* p. 37. Photocopy each child's letter to put in the special doily envelope. See **LG**. **(20)** <u>Jenga:</u> this a fully engaging way to review what is hard about grief for a kid and what a kid can do to help him or herself heal. The tower gets more and more fragile, just like us. We know it's going to fall. Keep the camera ready. Take a group photo with the rebuilt tower to put in a frame and autograph next time. **SNACK:** (Approximately **20** minutes) Dipped Pretzel Sticks **CLOSE:** (Approximately **15** minutes) <u>Session Log</u> *Someday Heaven*: **Review what we have learned about heaven.** <u>Take-Home Griefwork</u> <u>Happy Snaps</u> <u>Prayer</u>	**Handouts for Adults:** • Mel's Favorite Books • Feedback Form **Handouts for Kids:** • *Our Story* binders • Session Logs • Bible Verse Stickers • Feedback Form • Hug Coupons **Take-Home Griefwork:** OS p. 37– Write a "Special Letter" **Next Week:** • Celebrate or plan our "celebration." • Make a Pop-Up Puppet

NOTES

Check-In: use the white board die or a white board spinning wheel to land on a discussion topic (Amazon.) Let Wilma do the talking.

Shoes: I have a notebook with 32 pictures of pairs of shoes stored in plastic page protectors. The shoes represent different ages, lifestyles and activities. It is fun to "shop" for shoes. Check out my URL list at www.kidtalkgrief.com/ktbaccess. Spread them out on the floor and invite each child to find a pair of shoes that reminds them of the person who died. Stand on the shoes in a circle. Have each child explain why they picked that pair of shoes. Go around the circle again and ask each child to share what they would like to say to their decedent. Go around a third time and ask each child to share what their person would say back.

Love You Forever: *OS* p.36. List the ways to make love visible or memorialize. Examples: ring a bell, light a candle, place flowers by a photo or at the grave, wear or carry something that belonged to the person who died, donate in memory of your decedent, volunteer for a cause that was important to your loved one, eat a food they liked, write a letter, make a scrap book, work at something that would make your decedent proud.

Kid Talk Jenga: is played by the game rules. In addition, the child must name something they hate about having a broken heart or something that is hard about being a grieving kid. The tower becomes fragile – like us. We know at some point it will crumble - like us. It does. Take photos. Divide the blocks among the kids to rebuild the tower. It should not look like the original tower. (We are never the same again.) Before they place a block on the new structure, have them name something that they can do to heal or rebuild their lives, e.g. griefwork. Take a group photo with the completed tower for them to have as a souvenir. Note the new tower is much more interesting than the original. Grief can change us in a good way. Ask, "How has it changed you?"

A Special Letter: *OS* p. 37. This is a good-bye letter. It might say, "I remember…." Or, "I'm sorry…." Or, "I forgive you…." Or, "I wish that…." Or, whatever you would like to say to the person who died. Make photocopies of the children's letters so that each child can make a lovely envelope for his or her letter. Or supply special paper or stationery for copying the letter instead of photocopying it. The envelopes are made with 10" square doilies with a colorful 10" paper napkin placed underneath to show through. The corners are held together in the middle with a glue stick. Stickers may be applied to the envelopes to "seal" them closed.

Granola Pretzel Sticks: are a good seasonal snack. Place "candy melts" in a mug, the color of your choice, and microwave for 15 seconds at a time, stirring after each zap. Add a little coconut oil to make the candy thinner. Dip the pretzel sticks in vertically and allow them to drip before laying them down on wax paper. After a minute or so, roll them in granola, coconut, nuts, or sprinkles. As we heal, are we beginning to look and/or act differently? How?

Kid Talk Supply List – Week 12

- Handouts for Parents/Guardians: Book Resources, Adult's Feedback Form
- Handouts for Kids: Session Log and Bible Verse Stickers, Feedback Form, Hug Coupons
- Clipboard with Sign In Sheet, pen and WELCOME sign
- Name place cards and supplies to make one for new arrivals
- *Our Story* binder
- Ground Rules poster
- Book: *'Someday Heaven'* and box with question cards
- Glossary Cards from www.kidtalkgrief.com/ktbaccess
- Camera for taking photos of the kids
- Hand sanitizer

- Pencils
- Pens
- Markers
- Box of tissues
- Wilma, the tongue depressor puppet
- Basket of fiddle things (optional)
- Notebook of SHOES clipart
- Special Letter supplies include pretty paper or stationery, 10" square doilies, 10" colorful napkins, glue sticks, stickers.
- Modified *Our Story* p. 35 Treasured Memories. Refer to Leader's Guide p. 116. We prepare extras and trade with the children for what is in their binder.

- Jenga or Rainbow Tower building block game
- Snack: pretzel sticks, a glass or mug for each pair of kids to share, candy melts, coconut oil, granola or items of choice on plates into which you roll the dipped pretzel sticks.
- Plates and napkins
- Paper cups and ice water

Room Set Up: a tablecloth helps to identify the snack table.

Date: _____

Theme: 1. Heaven is our destiny. 2. Memorializing is making our love visible.

Series Scripture: *He heals the broken-hearted and binds up their wounds. Psalm 147:3.*

Scripture: Put scripture sticker here ➡
Revelations 21:4.

Pray:
Dear Lord, thank You that we can look forward to being in heaven forever. Thank You that we will never have a broken heart again when we are there with You.

My <u>favorite</u> activity about this session:

☐ Scriptures   ☐ Check-In with Wilma   ☐ Shoes   ☐ Love You Forever

☐ A Special Letter   ☐ Doily Envelope   ☐ Jenga Review   ☐ Snack – Dipped Pretzel Sticks

Explain your choice: _____

_____

What I want to remember from this session: _____

_____

_____

Signature _____

Mel's Favorite Books

CHRISTIAN TRADITION BOOKS FOR CHILDREN

Emily Lost Someone She Loved by Kathleen Fucci
God Gave Us Heaven by Lisa Tawn Bergren
Goodbye to Goodbyes A True Story About Jesus, Lazarus and an Empty Tomb by Lauren Chandler
Heaven for Kids by Randy Alcorn
In the Wake of Suicide: A Child's Journey by Diane Bouman Kaulen
Someday Heaven by Larry Libby
Someone I Love Died by Christine Harder Tangvald
Tell Me About Heaven by Randy Alcorn
When I'm With Jesus, For any Child with a Loved One in Heaven by Kimberly Rae

BOOKS FOR CHILDREN

A Garden Full of Butterflies by Lynn S. Combes
I Miss You, A First Look at Death by Pat Thomas
Something Very Sad Happened, A Toddler's Guide to Understanding Death by Bonnie Zucker
The Invisible String by Patrice Karst
When Dinosaurs Die: A Guide to Understanding Death by Laurie Krasny Brown and Mark Brown

BOOKS FOR TEENS

Modern Loss: Candid Conversation About Grief by Rebecca Soffer and Gabrielle Birkner
Saying Goodbye When You Don't Want To: Teens Dealing with Loss by Martha Bolton
Straight Talk About Death for Teenagers, How to Cope with Losing Someone You Love by Earl A. Grollman

BOOKS FOR ADULTS

50 Days of Heaven (Audio Book) Randy Alcorn Oasis Audio
But I Didn't Say Goodbye by B. Rubel (Helping children cope with suicide.)
Children and Grief by Joey O'Conner
Children Grieve Too: A Handbook for Parents of Grieving Children and Teens by Lauren Schneider, LCSW
Finding Your Way After the Suicide of Someone You Love by David B. Biebel, D. Min and Suzanne L. Foster, MA
How to Go on Living When Someone You Love Dies by Therese Rando
In the Wake of Suicide: A Child's Journey by Diane Bouman Kaulen
Within Heaven's Gates by Rebecca Springer
It's OK That You're Not OK, Meeting Grief and Loss in a Culture That Doesn't Understand by Megan Devine
It's Okay to Cry: A Parent's Guide to Helping Children Through the Losses of Life by H. Norman Wright
Tear Soup A Recipe for Healing After Loss by Pat Schwiebert and Chuck DeKlyen
The Loss That Is Forever: The Lifelong Impact of the Early Death of a Mother or Father by Maxine Harris
The Year of Magical Thinking by Joan Didion

Week 13: Hope and Celebration
See Leader's Guide for Details

Scripture & Theme	Activities (minutes) OS = *Our Story* Memory Book LG = Leader's Guide	Handouts and Take-Home Griefwork
Isaiah 40:51 *But those who hope in the Lord will renew their strength. They will soar on wings like eagles: they will run and not grow weary; they will walk and not be faint.* **Pray:** Dear Lord, thank You that You not only give us hope, but You also give us strength in hard times. Thank You for new friends at **Kid Talk**. **Theme:** We can have confidence that we are healing. We have lots of reasons to hope. We have learned how to do griefwork.	**OPEN:** (Approximately **25** minutes) **Welcome:** Ground Rules with poster <u>**Psalm 147: 3**</u> - ASL, discuss and pray. **Session Log:** Isaiah 40:51, discuss and pray. **Check-In: Glossary Match Review:** most matches wins. Do this activity if not using the time to plan the celebration. Otherwise, use Wilma to share her favorite **Kid Talk** activity. See **LG.** **FOCUS:** (Approximately **60** minutes) **(10) <u>Photo Review:</u>** do the photos help you to remember a favorite **Kid Talk** activity? See **LG.** **(10) <u>Plan a 10-minute Program for the Adults.</u>** **Plan Celebration** if having it next session. **(10) <u>When Someone Else Has a Broken Heart:</u>** OS p.38. **(25) <u>Make Wilma Puppets</u>:** use them to talk about what they have learned about grief, griefwork and heaven. **(5) <u>Stars</u>:** give each child a glow-in-the-dark star, a bit of putty, and a poem card. It is a reminder that even though we cannot see our decedents during the daytime, they are still there. **SNACK:** (Approximately **20** minutes) Strawberry Graham Cracker Bites **CLOSE:** (Approximately **15** minutes) <u>**Session Log**</u> – last one. **Kid Talk Feed-Back Form:** have the kids complete the form and turn it in to you. **Love Bubbles:** send love to our decedents by saying, "I love you,_____," and blowing bubbles. Any message can be spoken out loud before blowing bubbles. Soon the room is filled with "love bubbles." We can blow bubbles for each other, too. **Bell Chime:** one last message to our decedents. **Prayer**	**Handouts for Adults:** • Adult's Feedback Form (extras) • Parting Song • Schedule for next **Kid Talk** Support Group Series **Handouts for Kids:** • *Our Story* binders • Session Logs • Bible Verse Stickers • **Kid Talk** Feedback Forms (extras) • Parting Song • Group Photo **Take-Home Griefwork:** None. Unless there is some prep work for our celebration. **Next Week: (MAYBE)** We will celebrate our God who heals, **Kid Talk**, new friends and the fact that we have learned how to do griefwork!

NOTES

Check-In Review: look through the Session Log pages, inviting the kids to remember what they liked or learned. Afterwards, give them a Feedback Form to complete, or save it for the close if you prefer. This might be a good time for the kids to decide what they would like to share with the adults. Suggestion: ASL Psalm 147:3 and share a favorite page from *Our Story.* Some of the kids may be comfortable sharing what they liked best about **Kid Talk** or something important they learned about grief.

Glossary Match Game: a glossary of the "language of grief" terms starts on p. 148 through p. 151. Avery compatible PDF cards for the match game are on the website: www.kidtalkgrief.com/ktbaccess. This makes a good team game. Print the cards, cut them apart and laminate them. Select which cards you would like to use. Invite the children to matchthem up. Most correct matches win.

Wilma Pop-Up Puppets are made with three tongue depressors, " squares (or triangles) of fake fur, googly eyes, 1" pieces of hook and loop Velcro, pipe cleaners, pieces of stick-on colored foam ¾" x 2" and extra fine red and black permanent markers for the eyes and mouths. Tiny pom-poms can be added for the noses. Invite the children to have their puppets share with the adults. DIY directions are included with this week's material.

Glow-in-the-Dark Stars: can be found at local toy departments. Print a card in color on Avery business cards at www.kidtalkgrief.com/ktbaccess. Provide putty the children can use to stick a star on the card and then on the ceiling of their room or place of choice.

Twinkle, twinkle little star so true,
you bring brightness to my life
when I'm thinking of you.

When Someone Else Has a Broken Heart: *OS* p. 38. It is good to think about ways we can be a caring presence for somebody else who is grieving the death of someone important to them. The pictures suggest some ways we can show that we care. How else could we be a friend? This page is available in color as a PDF at www.kidtalkgrief.com/ktbaccess.

Strawberry Graham Cracker Bites: can be found at: www.allrecipes.com/recipe/233226/strawberry-graham-cracker-bites.

Love Bubbles: 1-oz. colorful little bottles can be purchased with party supplies very inexpensively. Make self-adhesive labels that say, "**Kid Talk.**" These are available to print at www.kidtalkgrief.com/ktbaccess.   Let the kids stick them on the bottles and then fill the room with "love bubbles."   Stand in a circle and say, "I love you,_____!" and then blow bubbles. Include everyone in the group, not just the decedents. "Toast" one another too.

Kid Talk Feedback Form: is included with this week's material. It allows the children to "grade" their **Kid Talk** experience with a letter after each of the six statements, or by writing the number of the statement in the appropriate place (in their opinion), on the target. Note: the parents are also given feedback forms to complete at this session.

Bear Hug Coupons: PDF printable Bear Hug coupons from www.printthistoday.com. The kids may give them out this week or next if you are planning a 14th week celebration.

Strawberry Graham Cracker Bites

- Handouts for Parents/Guardians: Adult's Feedback Forms (extras), Parting Song, Schedule for next **Kid Talk** Series
- Handouts for Kids: Session Log and Bible Verse Stickers, Kid's Feedback Forms (extras), Parting Song
- Clipboard with Sign-In Sheet, pen and WELCOME sign
- Supplies to make a name place card for new arrivals
- ***Our Story*** binder
- Glossary Cards from www.kidtalkgrief.com/ktbaccess
- Group photo to mount on a page for autographing
- PowerPoint Photo Collage of **Kid Talk** CD
- Hand sanitizer

• Pencils • Pens • Markers • Box of tissues • Glossary Match Cards for review of the language of grief • Wilma puppet making supplies: tongue depressors, triangles of fur for hair, googly eyes, mini pom-pom for the nose, extra fine red and black permanent markers for eyes and mouth, ¾" x 2" strips of sticky backed foam, ¾" piece of self-stick hook and loop tape, and two pieces of pipe-cleaner 6½"	• Glow-in-the-dark stars, tacky putty, poem on printed cards. • 1-oz. Bubbles with **Kid Talk** labels • Bell Chime • Bear Hug Coupons • Strawberry Graham Cracker Bites: fresh strawberries, whipped cream in a can, Nutella, blueberries, Teddy Grahams, plastic knives • Plates and napkins • Paper cups and ice water

Room Set Up: a tablecloth helps to identify the snack table.

Kid Talk Session Log – Week 13

Date: _____

Theme We can have confidence that we are healing. We have lots of reasons to hope and to celebrate!

Series Scripture: *He heals the broken-hearted and binds up their wounds. Psalm 147:3.*

Scripture: Put scripture sticker here ➡
Isaiah 40:51

Pray:
Dear Lord, thank You that You not only give us hope, but You also give us strength in the hard times. Thank You for helping me to do griefwork. Thank You for my new friends at Kid Talk.

My <u>favorite</u> activity about this session:

☐ Scriptures   ☐ *Our Story* Review   ☐ Photo Collage   ☐ Making a Puppet

☐ Stars   ☐ Glossary Match Game   ☐ Love Bubbles   ☐ Snack – Strawberry Graham Bites

Explain your choice: _____

_____

What I want to remember from this session: _____

_____

_____

Signature _____

How satisfied are you with **Kid Talk**? Did we get close to the bull's eye in meeting your needs and expectations? Please give us a grade from "A" to "F" by putting the number from each statement below on the target. Or you can just put the letter grade at the end of each of the six statements. Thank you!

1. I understand more about grief.

2. I was able to share my feelings with others.

3. I could talk about the person who died.

4. I came away with ideas of things to do to help heal my grief.

5. I learned about God.

6. The leaders were helpful.

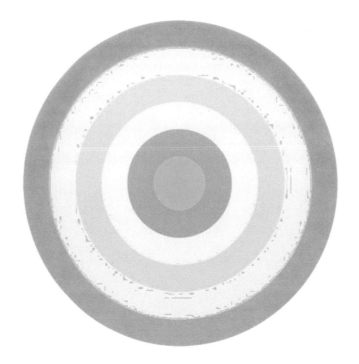

What was the most important thing that you learned?

_____

_____

Pop-Up Puppet – Activity

DIY Instructions with Photos at www.kidtalkgrief.com/ktbaccess

Supplies Needed:	Materials for Construction:
Ruler/Scissors	3 - 6" wood tongue depressors (A, B and C)*
Fine sandpaper	1" of ½" wide self-stick hook tape
Pencil	1 ½" x 1 ½" piece of self-stick foam, any color
Toothpicks to apply glue	2 - pipe cleaners twisted together and cut to 6 ½ "
White glue	2 - ¼" pony beads for hands
Glue gun (optional)	1 - 7mm pom-pom for the nose (optional)
Red and black extra fine point permanent markers	2 - small googly eyes
	1" square piece of fur: *(Note: Draw square on back of the fur fabric. Cut along the line with the <u>tips</u> of very sharp scissors, cutting only through the fabric and then pulling away the cut piece to leave the fur intact.)*

*Any size craft sticks will work. Adjust body parts to scale. However, tongue depressors work best because they are made from quality wood.

Instructions:

1. Head: Cut off 1 ¼" of tongue depressor **A**. This is the head. Sand the cut edge to make it smooth.

2. Back: Glue head to top of tongue depressor **B**. This is the back of the puppet. The Velcro will be attached to the underside of this piece.

3. Apply hook tape to the <u>back side</u> of tongue depressor **B** about 1 ¼" from the bottom edge. (See 2.)

4. Front: Cut off ¼ "of tongue depressor **C**. This will be the <u>bottom front</u> of the puppet. Sand the cut edge. Place it so the straight edges of **A** (head) and **C** (bottom front) meet for the mouth. The bottom edge of **C** will extend beyond the back (**B**).

5. On the paper side of the foam, draw a line ½" from each end. Carefully lift up the paper and cut it away ½". This leaves paper in the middle and sticky surfaces on the sides. The paper allows the stick B to slide so the puppet can talk. Center the paper side of the foam about a half inch below the top of stick **C**, leaving room to draw the mouth. Wrap the sticky foam ends to meet center back of stick **B**. This allows you to put your thumb on the Velcro and push the back stick (**B**) up and down to make the puppet talk.

6. Draw the mouth of the puppet with the bottom lip at the top edge of **C** and the top lip on **A**. Add eyes, nose, and eyebrows as desired. Glue on googly eyes. Push the bottom stick (**B**) up and extend the mouth to look open. Add a tongue, teeth, epiglottis as desired.

7. Twist together 2 pipe cleaners. Glue a pony bead to each end for hands. Center and glue the arms to the back of B on the foam about 3/8" from the top edge. Bring the arms around to the front of the puppet.

8. Spread a thin layer of glue to the back of the fur. Center the hair in place, wrapping it from the back of the head to the front. (Place it about ¼ "above the top of the head and bring the corners together in front.

Visit www.facebook.com/planetofthepuppets for inspiration to create your puppet or purchase a kit to make 12 Pop-Up Puppets at: www.etsy.com/listing/293313237/pop-up-puppet-kit-planet-of-the-puppets.

Parting Song

(tune Edelweiss)

May the Lord, our mighty God
Bless and keep you forever,
Grant you peace, perfect peace,
Strength in every endeavour.
Lift up your eyes and see His face
And His grace forever.
May the Lord, our mighty God
Bless and keep you forever.

Kid Talk Adult's Feedback

To help us better meet your child's needs, please complete and return this questionnaire.
Answers will be held as confidential and used only to evaluate and enhance this program.

Dates:_____Facilitator/s: _____

QUESTIONS	A	B	C	D	F
1. My child gained understanding of the grieving process.					
2. My child seems more comfortable with his/her grief.					
3. My child is better able to talk about the person who died.					
4. My child has obtained strategies for coping with his or her grief.					
5. My child has grown to understand how scripture brings comfort.					
6. My child has a clearer understanding of heaven as described in the Bible.					
7. Facilitator(s) provided appropriate guidance and leadership.					
8. What do you think was most helpful for your child?					
9. What topic would you like to have covered?					
10. What improvements would you suggest?					
11. Would you recommend Kid Talk to others dealing with loss?	YES		NO		

Week 14: Celebration!

Scripture & Theme	Activities (minutes) OS = *Our Story* Memory Book LG = Leader's Guide	Handouts and Take-Home Griefwork
Psalm 147:3 *He heals the broken hearted and binds up their wounds.* **Pray:** Dear Lord, thank You for being our healer and our friend, for giving us the healing process of grief for **Kid Talk**, and our new friends. Thank You for always being there for us and for the hope of heaven.	**OPEN:** (Approximately **25** minutes) **Welcome:** Ground Rules with poster Psalm 147:3. ASL, discuss and pray. **Check-In:** <u>Photo Review:</u> (Yes, again.) What do you see in the photo review that you'd like to share with the adults? **FOCUS:** (Approximately **45** minutes) **Glossary Match Review:** Most matches wins. **Frames:** each child paints/decorates a frame for a photo souvenir from **Kid Talk**. **SNACK:** (Approximately **20** minutes) Seasonal, pizza, or Kid's Choice. **CLOSE:** (Approximately **10** minutes) Join adult group, show **Kid Talk** photo collage and share favorite activities from **Kid Talk**. **Distribute Hug Coupons.**	**Handouts for Adults:** Parting Song (if this is the last meeting) **Handouts for Kids:** • Hug Coupons • CD of **Kid Talk** Photo Collage

Suggested CELEBRATION SCHEDULE:	**Suggested Children's Program for Adults:**
6:30 p.m. Pizza! 7:00 p.m. Adult Talk and **Kid Talk** 8:10 p.m. Children present their program for the Adults. 8:25 p.m. Children distribute "Hug Coupons." 8:30 p.m. Consider closing with *"The Parting Song"* It is sung to the tune of Edelweiss.	1. ASL Psalm 147:3 2. Present photo slide show. 3. *Invite children to share about their favorite OS page or activity.* 4. Invite children to share what they liked best about **Kid Talk**. Consider having puppets talk. (Summarize Feedback forms.)

NOTES

Appendix

Kid Talk - Activity Locator

Locate the description and directions for any activity in the **Kid Talk Curriculum** or *Our Story* **Memory Book**. A list of **Printable PDFs** available at www.kidtalkgrief.com/ktbaccess can be found on Page 141.

ACTIVITY	WEEK	KTC PAGE	OS PAGE	ON WEB
A Special Letter	12	114, 115, 116 137	37	
About the Death	3	47, 48	16	
Acrostics – Orientation Week	O - 3	20, 23. 40, 41	11, 12	
All About Me	1	33, 34	8	
Alphabet Poem	2	40, 41	13, 14	
Anger Thermometer	6	73, 74, 80	-	√
ASL Psalm 147:3	ALL	20, 21, 93, 94	-	√
Bear Hug Coupons	13	121, 122, 133	-	√
Bell Chime	3 +	47, 49, 133	-	
Bouquet of Memories	10	103, 104, 105	33	
Bracelets	1 +	35, 137	-	
Bumper Stickers	7	82, 83	-	
Butterfly Coloring Sheets	3, 10 +	48, 103, 107, 134	-	
Butterfly Craft	10	104, 105	-	
Check-In with a Dice	1, 9	18, 34, 35, 36, 96, 97, 115	-	
Check-In with Paperclip Chain	4	18, 53, 54	-	
Check-In with Pop-Up Pirate	3	18, 47, 48	-	
Check in with Rock, Paper, Scissors	10	103	-	
Check-In with Toilet Paper	2	18, 40, 41	-	
Check-In Volcano Report	6	18, 73, 74, 79	-	
Check-In Weather Report	5	18, 61	-	
Coloring Pages, Mandalas and Mazes	ALL	134	-	
Chutes and Ladders	8	87, 88, 134	-	
Craft Stick Exercise	1	33, 34	-	
Doily Envelopes	12	114, 115, 116, 141	37	
Dream Catchers	9	95, 96, 98, 100	-	
Dreams	9	95, 96, 98, 101	29	
Duck	0	23	3	
Emily Lost Someone She Loved	0	20, 24, 118	-	
Favorite Things	1	40, 41	10	
Feedback Forms	13	119, 121, 124, 127	-	
Feelings Cards and Vase	5	61, 62, 65, 74, 134	23	√
Feelings of Grief Word Search	4	53, 58	-	
Fiddle Things to Check In	0	20, 22	-	
Flannel Board	3	47, 48, 53	-	√
Flash Paper	0	20, 23, 134	-	

Kid Talk - Activity Locator

ACTIVITY	WEEK	KTC PAGE	OS PAGE	ON WEB
Funeral/Memorial Service	3	47, 48	17	
GAK	8	87, 88, 89, 91	-	
Glossary Match Game (Language of Grief)	13	21, 26, 119, 120, 148 - 151	-	√
Glow-In-The-Dark Stars	13	119, 120, 122, 135	-	
Grief Behaviors (Mourning)	5	61, 64	24	
Grief Tips for Kids and Teens	5	61, 63, 68-70	26	√
Grief Vomit Bags	6	73, 74	-	
Griefwork	5, 7	9, 12, 61, 63, 64, 68-70, 75, 82	26	
Ground Rules	0 +	20, 21, 28	-	√
Happy Snaps	1 +	33, 35	-	
How My Family Has Changed	8	87, 88	27	
Imprints – Your Mark on My Life	8	87, 88	28	
Kid Talk Jenga	12	114, 115	-	
Love Bubbles	13	119, 121	-	√
Love You Forever	11	114, 115	36	
Marshmallow Shooter	7	82, 83, 84, 86, 135	-	
Meet My _____	1	33, 40, 41	9	
Memory Box	12	108, 109, 110, 135	-	
Model Magic	0	20, 24	-	
Mosaic Heart Coloring Page	1	22, 26, 134	-	
Mouth Coil Rainbow Streamer	4	53, 54	-	
"Move!"	0	20, 22, 29	-	
My Circle of Support	9	95, 96	30	
My Personal Experience with Death	3	47, 48	15	
My Feelings of Grief	5	59, 61, 62, 63	23	
My Grief Bundle	4	53, 54	20	
My Gratitude List	11	108, 109	34	
My Safe Place	9	95, 97	31	
My Silent Hurting Heart	0	20, 23, 24, 30	6, 7	
Name Place Holders	ALL	17, 140	-	
No Bake Cookies	5	61, 64, 65, 67	-	
Paint Rocks	2	40, 42, 43	-	
Parting Song	13	119, 126	-	
Persian Petition for Reconciliation	6	73, 75, 81	-	
Photo Intros of Decedents	1, 2	33, 40, 41	9	
Pop Corn with No Lid	6	73, 76	-	
Pop-Up Pirate	3	18, 47, 48, 136	-	
Power Point Kid Talk Collage	13	18, 119	-	

ACTIVITY	WEEK	KTC PAGE	OS PAGE	ON WEB
Scream Boxes	6	73, 76, 136	-	
Scriptures Basket	8	87, 88, 92, 93	-	√
Session Log	ALL	21		√
Shoes	12	114, 115, 136	-	√
Smile on a Stick Photo	0, 1	20, 24, 136	-	
Snack (object lesson or fits theme)	ALL	24, 138	-	
Someday Heaven	ALL	20, 24, 31	-	√
Tangled Ball of Emotions – Coloring	4	54, 59	-	
Tangled Ball of Emotions – Yarn Toss	4	54, 55	-	
Tear Soup Book/Video	1	33, 34, 133	-	
Tears in a Bottle	1	33, 35, 36	-	√
Tears Poem	0, 1	20, 33, 35	5	√
The Pain of Grief	4	53, 55	21	
Tickets	1	35	-	
Toilet Bowl Love	6	73, 75, 82, 83	25	
Treasured Memories/Floral Stones	5, 6	63, 73, 108, 109	-	
Treasured Memories/Treasure Chest	11	108, 109, 110, 112, 135	35	
Triangle Book	4	53, 55, 56, 60	-	
Uniquely Me	1	33, 34, 39	-	
Volcano of Feelings	5	73, 74, 79	-	
Votive Battery Candles	3	47, 48	18, 19	
Watermelon Hugs	5	47, 49, 52, 61, 64	22	
"We Remember Them"	3	47	18	
"We Will Light Candles"	3	47, 48	19	√
When Someone Else Has a Broken Heart	12	119, 121	38	
Where Do You Stand?	1	33, 34, 38	-	
Will I Heal?	10	103, 104	32	
Wilma, Pop-Up Puppet	0 + 13 (DIY)	20, 22, 26, 40, 87, 95, 108, 109, 119, 120, 125, 136	-	
Wilted Rose	7	82, 83, 137	-	

Kid Talk Supply Pantry

See www.kidtalkgrief.com/ktbaccess

You will need general craft supplies.
If you choose to do all the Kid Talk activities, you will need the following:

Avery Labels: numbers 5160 and 5395 or their equivalents. These are address labels (1"x 2 5/8", 30 labels per sheet) and adhesive name badges, respectively. Address labels say "**Kid Talk**" and are used to label Tears in a Bottle (Week 1), Triangle Book (Week 4), Scream Boxes (Week 6), GAK baggies (Week 8), Cigar Boxes (Week 11) and Love Bubbles (Week 14). Adhesive name badges are used for Scripture verses, "We Will Light Candles" (Week 3), and "Stars" poem (Week 14).

Baggies: a variety of sizes are useful to have on hand for taking home projects or snacks.

Basket: a small one, 4" to 6", for passing around assorted laminated cards used as springboards for dialogue.

Beaded Bracelet Supplies: beading elastic, assorted pony beads and alphabet beads. This is a "stand-by" craft to use as needed. It is a favorite activity. The kids love finding the letters of their decedent's name for their bracelets. We do run out of the letters needed for "I love."

Bear Hug Coupons: this is my favorite website for free "printables." They are for your personal use only. Maryam's beautiful work, including children's coloring pages can also be found at Facebook on the link below:

www.printthistoday.com/wp-content/uploads/2013/01/love-coupons-2.png
Facebook link at: www.facebook.com/groups/515838331927882/

Bell Chime:

www.amazon.com/Zenergy-Teachers-Classroom-Management
Meditation/dp/B0811KHJMT/ref=sr_1_47?dchild=1&keywords=bell+chime&qid=1587
580575&sr=8-47#customerReviews

Books: (A list is included with Week 12 on p. 118.)
'Emily Lost Someone She Loved' by Kathleen Fucci ISBN -13: 978-0-9909622-0-5
'Someday Heaven' by Larry Libby ISBN 978-0-310-70105-7
'Tear Soup' by Pat Schwiebert and Chuck DeKlyen ISBN 0-9615197-6-2
'When I'm With Jesus' by Kimberly Rae ISBN 13: 978-1484081730
'The Invisible String' by Patrice Karst ISBN 9780-316-48623-1 (pbk)
'Goodbye to Goodbyes' by Lauren Chandler ISBN 9781-784-983-772

Chutes and Ladders Board Game (and extra multi-color pawn pieces):

www.walmart.com/ip/Assorted-1-Inch-Multi-Color-Pawns-Pieces-for-Board-Games-Component-Tabletop-Markers-Arts-Crafts-24-Pack-by-Super-Z-Outlet/233955697

Coloring Pages:

- **Butterflies:** www.supercoloring.com/coloring-pages/insects/butterfly?page=1
- **Mandalas:** www.supercoloring.com/coloring-pages/arts-culture/mandala
- **Mazes:** www.trendenterprises.com/collections/free-printables/type_maze **AND** www.thesprucecrafts.com/free-printable-mazes-for-kids-1357612
- **Mosaic Heart:**
  i.pinimg.com/736x/9a/15/5f/9a155fdfe09259043a1caa2ac4940591--color-art-art-reference.jpg
- www.pinterest.com - **is the best resource.**

Dice: standard 6-sided dice *and* dice with colored sides. (Amazon)

Feelings Vase Activity Supplies:

- Clear glass bud vase with bulb shape base easily found at a thrift shop
- 32 Feelings Cards - with subscription to www.kidtalkgrief.com/ktbaccess
- Set of Liquid Food Coloring (4) by McCormick or Watsons
- 4-oz empty contact lens solution bottle to contain bleach

Floral stones in a small metal container. The lid is used as a tray to pass around the little bottles of food coloring.

Flash Paper:

www.dreamlandmagic.com/products/flashpaper?gclid=CjwKCAjw1v_0BRAkEiwALFkj5lXcblID2Yv0CqkzEYseI6m8m_aOsmcmUaU7V46Kzd93tgWVQitFhhoCHyUQAvD_BwE

Fiddle Things: pecans, polished stones, small hearts cut out of fleece and more. Google "fidget toys" to discover lots of possibilities. We have found that coloring works best with younger kids.

Foam Dry Erase Block:

www.amazon.com/Mind-Sparks-Foam-Erase-Blocks/dp/B017BCPWN4

Glow in the Dark Stars: easily found online or big box stores.

www.amazon.com/Glow-In-The-Dark-Stars/dp/B004OZGLGY

Handouts for the kids are included with the weekly materials or Leader's Guide. A few items you will want to print from the website at www.kidtalkgrief.com. A list of Handouts for Adults is found in the Appendix with the URLs for copyrighted articles. Alternative handouts can be found in Online Resources on p. 113.

Jenga Classic Game: easily found online or big box stores.

Marshmallow Shooters: instructions are included with Week 7 on p. 86.

www.artofmanliness.com/articles/make-marshmallow-shooter/

Memory Box Supplies:

- Cigar Boxes can be obtained at local smoke shops.
- Mod Podge Gloss or white glue
- Sponge brushes
- Pictures and words cut from magazines. It helps to have them in different colored folders to share around the table.
- Different colored folders for clippings makes sharing easier

Model Magic: Crayola Model Magic White, Modeling Clay Alternative found at craft supply, big-box stores or online.

Mouth Coil: found on Amazon under magic supplies: Doowops Mouth Coils Vomit Paper, Magic Tricks Stage Magic Accessories.

Place Card Holder: Mini Sign Display Holder Price Card Tag Label - Countertop Stand Case 7cm x 4cm (30) found on Amazon or a Dollar Store.

Pop-Up Pirate: a toy similar to Jack-in-the-Box, can be found on Amazon under toys.

Wilma, Pop-Up Puppet:

Pop-Up Puppets* can be seen on www.facebook.com/planetofthepuppets. Purchase kits to make 12 pop-up puppets at: www.etsy.com/listing/293313237/pop-up-puppet-kit-planet-of-the-puppets. DIY instructions are found on p. 129. Instructions with photos are on our website at: www.kidtalkgrief.com.

*Thanks are due to Rob H. D'Arc, creator of Pop-Up Puppets for granting us permission to publish our DIY instructions for making them.

Scream Box Supplies:

- Shoe Box (one per child)
- Paper towel tube or a heavy cardboard tube from wrapping paper cut into 12" lengths
- Newspapers – lots.
- Colored Duct Tape

Shoes Clip Art Notebook: printable clip art of an assortment of shoes, print them and put them in sheet protectors in a notebook. Distribute them around the room on the floor. Invite the kids to choose a pair to stand on and talk to their decedent. Find a list of shoe clip art URLs at www.kidtalkgrief.com/ktbaccess.

Smile-on-a-Stick:

www.reubenmiller.typepad.com/my_weblog/2008/06/smile-on-a-stic.html

Special Letter Envelopes:

Pretty stationery or special paper (Dollar Store)
10" colorful party napkins
10" Square Doilies (200 Pack for $11.99)

Toy Flushing Toilet Magnet: our ACME Magnetic Toilet that makes a flushing sound was purchased in 1998. You may find one on EBAY. Hasbro made a Real Sound Flushing Toilet Game that also squirts water, also may be found on EBAY. A gag greeting card is another option. YouTube has a "Toilet Flushing Sound Effect." Imagination and pantomime may have to suffice.

Votive Candles: battery operated. Easily found at big box stores.

Wilting Flower:

www.magictricks.com/drooping-flower.html

Disclaimer:

The Internet is dynamic, therefore web addresses or links contained in this book may have changed since publication and so may no longer be valid.

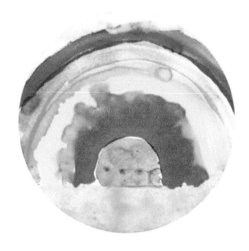

Kid Talk - Snack List

SNACK	WK	URL for RECIPE
Ants on A Log (6 variations)	2	www.foodnetwork.com/recipes/packages/recipes-for-kids/cooking-with-kids/reinvented--ants-on-a-log
Apple and Grape Turtles	8	kitchenfunwithmy3sons.com/wp-content/uploads/2011/03/Apple-Turtle-Snacks-000.907.jpg
Apple Sandwiches	9	thriftyjinxy.com/apple-sandwiches-recipe-great-school-snack/
Banana caterpillar	3	www.sheknows.com/food-and-recipes/articles/990449/3-creepy-crawly-kids-snacks/
Banana Palm Trees	11	www.mommysfabulousfinds.com/fruit-palm-tree-how-to-get-kids-to-eat-fruit/
Butterfly Snacks Bags	10	thesimpleparent.com/butterfly-snack-bags/
Crunchy Apple Boats		grandiose.net/kids-recipes/crunchy-apple-boats/
Dulce de Leche with Apple Wedges	1	www.seriouseats.com/recipes/2015/02/dulce-de-leche-recipe.html
Flowerpot Pudding Cups	10	www.readyseteat.com/recipes-Flower-Pot-Pudding-Cups-7821
Fruit and Vegetable Bunny Snack		www.forkly.com/food/9-healthy-and-fun-easter-snacks-for-kids/
Graham Cracker Band Aids	4	kidfriendlythingstodo.com/make-graham-cracker-band-aids-for-a-fun-halloween-treat-a-kid-friendly-thing-to-do/
Healthy No-bake Granola Bites	5	www.melskitchencafe.com/no-bake-healthy-granola-bites/
Individual Fruit Pizzas	12	www.foodnetwork.com/recipes/ree-drummond/individual-fruit-pizzas-recipe-2008593
Mexican Tortilla Pinwheels		www.dinneratthezoo.com/wprm_print/7166
Mini Brownie Turkeys		www.allrecipes.com/recipe/276135/mini-brownie-turkeys/
Ritz Cracker Sandwich	9	www.makeandtakes.com/cream-cheese-jam-cracker-snacks
Strawberry Graham Cracker Bites	13	www.allrecipes.com/recipe/233226/strawberry-graham-cracker-bites/
Valentine's or Christmas Cookies		sallysbakingaddiction.com/best-sugar-cookies/ Provide edible ink pens for kids to color their cookies.

Please follow CDC recommendations for food safety at:
www.cdc.gov/foodsafety/newsletter/food-safety-and-Coronavirus.html

Kid Talk Curriculum - Handouts for Adults
Parents' Weekly Resources

Orientation: "**Kid Talk** – Objectives" (**Kid Talk** Curriculum p. 12)

Week 1   *Helping Children Cope with Grief* by Alan D. Wolfelt, Ph.D.*
www.centerforloss.com/2016/12/helping-children-cope-grief

Week 2   *Is My Child's Grief Normal*? by Mel Erickson
12 Simple Tips & Tools To Help Your Grieving Child by Mel Erickson, Amazon.com.

Week 3   *Helping Children with Funerals* by Alan D. Wolfelt, Ph.D.*
www.centerforloss.com/2016/12/helping-children-funerals

Helping Children Understand Cremation
www.centerforloss.com/2016/12/helping-children-understand-cremation

Watermelon Hugs

Week 4   *Helping Teenagers Cope with Grief* by Alan D. Wolfelt, Ph.D.*
www.centerforloss.com/2016/12/helping-teenagers-cope-grief

Week 5   *Sibling Survivor Guilt* by Bob Baugher, Ph.D. **

Week 6   Anger Thermometer

Week 7   Instructions for making a Marshmallow Shooter

Week 8   Scripture Verses for the Bereaved

Week 9   *Understanding Nightmares* by Bob Baugher, Ph.D. **

Week 10 "Helping a Grandparent Who Is Grieving" by Alan D. Wolfelt, Ph.D.
www.centerforloss.com/2016/12/helping-grandparent-grieving

Week 11 Online Resources

Week 12 Book Resources

Week 13 Schedule for next **Kid Talk** Support Group Series
Parting Song
Adult's Feedback Form

*All articles by Dr. Wolfelt can be found at: www.centerforloss.com/category/articles
**Articles by Dr. Baugher can be found at: www.bobbaugher.com

Email Template - Example

DATE: _____

TO: Parents and Guardians (and sometimes Kids!)

FROM: (facilitators' names)

RE: **Kid Talk** Week _____

Greetings Parents and Guardians!

Our theme last week was_____.

A highlight of our time together was_____.

Our take-home griefwork is_____.

Next week our theme is_____. Our activities will include_____.

Affirmation:_____.

Salutation:_____.

SAMPLE EMAIL

DATE: (One or two days before the group meets.)

TO: (email address)

FROM: Ms. Mel and **Kid Talk** Team

RE: **Kid Talk** Week 1

Greetings Parents, Guardians and Kids!

Last week was our get acquainted session and our theme was "my broken heart." We loved the sculptures the kids made from Model Magic! They will paint them this week as we learn more about each other: how we are unique (*Our Story* page 8 and a "puzzle" interview) and the same (Game: Where Do I Stand?). It will be fun to see the "smile on a stick" photos that illustrate how we may look happier than we feel.

We will talk about tears and collect our "tears in a bottle." We will share photos of our loved ones and use page 9 of *Our Story* to introduce them. Next week we will get better acquainted with our decedents (new word!) using the acrostics on page 12 of *Our Story* and Favorite Things on page 10. Your child may need your help filling in the blanks. Thank you for contributing to his or her memory work. We love that you will be processing memories together. It is healing for both of you!

It is a privilege for us to walk with your kids through this difficult time. Please feel free to call us if you have any questions or concerns. Our contact info is on your **Kid Talk** Schedule.

Remember, *He heals the brokenhearted and binds up their wounds.* Psalm 147:3 (It is our theme verse. We begin each session by signing it with ASL!)

See you at 6:25 p.m. on Wednesday!

Ms. Mel and team

PDF Printables

Found at www.kidtalkgrief.com/ktbaccess
(*free to owners of* **Kid Talk** *Curriculum*)

14-Week Overview of **Kid Talk** Curriculum	Weekly
ASL video of Psalm 147:3	Weekly
Feelings Cards	Week 6
Funeral Story Flannel Board	Week 3
Kid Talk Binder Labels (for 1' 3-ring binders)	
"**Kid Talk**" Labels (for projects)	
Language of Grief – Glossary Cards	Weekly
Love Bubbles Labels ("**Kid Talk**" – Avery printable)	Week 13
Roster (sample template)	
Scripture Verse Cards (Avery printable)	Week 8
Scripture Verse Stickers (Avery printable)	Weekly
Shoe Pictures	Week 12
Sign-In Sheet (sample template)	Weekly
Someday Heaven topics (Avery printable)	Weekly
Star Poem (Avery printable)	Week 13
Tears in a Bottle Label (Psalm 56:8 – Avery printable)	Week 2
"We Will Light Candles" (Avery printable stickers)	Week 3

Sample Forms

Kid Talk Roster (Sample Template)
Winter/Spring 2020

PARENTS/GUARDIANS:

	NAME	EMAIL	PHONE	CHILDREN
1				
2				
3				
4				
5				
6				
7				
8				

KIDS:

	NAME	WHO DIED	DOD	CAUSE OF DEATH	BIRTHDAY	GRADE	ALLERGIES OR CONCERNS
1							
2							
3							
4							
5							
6							
7							
8							

Kid Talk - Registration (Sample)

Date:_____ Phone: (home)_____(cell) _____

Email: _____

Adult/Family Name/Address	Teen Names/D of B/Grade	Children Names/D of B/Grade
_____	_____	_____
_____	_____	_____
_____	_____	_____
Name of Deceased/Relationship	Date of Death	Cause of Death

Does the child (children) know the complete cause of death? _____   Who informed them?_____   Did the child (children) participate in family rituals (i.e. funeral) at the time of the death? _____   What specifically?
Have there been other losses as a result of the death? (moves, school changes, home life, support network)
What are you experiencing at this time that is the most difficult for your family?
Are there health/life concerns at this time? (sleeping, eating, school performance, illness, suicidal tendencies, risk taking)
Do you have specific problems with your children? Do your children have special needs or medication?
What would you like to see happen for your child (children) at **Kid Talk**? Please be specific.
What is your child (children's) church experience?

Support Group Agreement (Sample)

> Support Group Agreement
> For **"Kid Talk"** Bereavement Support Group

The **"Kid Talk"** series in which_____is enrolled, will meet for fourteen (14) sessions at the following times & location:

Day: _____

Time: _____

Location: _____

Facilitators: _____and_____

I,_____, **understand that:**

(Please print first and last name.)

1. The purpose of the group is to help my child work through the normal grief process.
2. What and how much he/she shares is up to him/her. He/she always has the right to pass.
3. Every reasonable effort will be made to maintain confidentiality about all aspects of his/her participation in the group; however, confidentiality cannot be guaranteed due to the participatory nature of a support group. If he/she chooses to disclose information that indicates a danger of harm to him/herself or others, then the facilitator will be obliged to report it.
4. Homework, referred to as "take-home griefwork," may be assigned. These exercises have been found to help other persons work through their grief. I will encourage my child to complete these assignments.
5. **Kid Talk** facilitators are not therapists and do <u>not</u> offer psychological counseling or therapy but offer education and support on the topic of grief. If the **Kid Talk** leaders think that your child has complicated grief which requires therapeutic intervention, the parent/guardian will be given a referral to a mental health professional.
6. If my child is in counseling or therapy, it is my responsibility to notify the counselor of his/her participation in **Kid Talk**.
7. If unable to attend a session, I will notify a facilitator or someone in the group before the meeting.
8. I may call any time with questions or concerns at:

_____,

_____   _____.

Signature of Parent or Guardian   **Date**

Disclosure/Permission Statement (Sample)

Kid Talk is a faith-based bereavement support group series for children sponsored by:

_____. This fourteen-week support group experience is designed to help your child deal with loss due to death. It is not intended to diagnose or treat any mental health problem (e.g. depression, chronic mental illness). The environment is meant to be supportive and educational. In this informal setting we are not able to evaluate the needs of your child concerning any mental health issues. If you or your children are having significant problems dealing with your daily activities, we encourage you to consult with a physician or counselor for help, and we would be happy to provide referrals. The **Kid Talk** facilitators are not liable for any problems (e.g. memories, sleep or eating problems, health problems) your child may experience while attending or after completion of this support group series. If you are concerned regarding how this may impact your child's, physical or mental health, please consult with your physician. We are always willing to discuss with you your concerns about your child's grieving process and what may or may not be "normal."

Location: _____

Cost: A much appreciated $20 donation will help subsidize the cost of the *Our Story* **Memory Book**, handouts, craft supplies and snacks used or consumed during the 14 sessions. Payments and/or scholarships can be arranged.

Facilitators: The **Kid Talk** Facilitators are retired professionals and/or vetted volunteers trained to work with grieving youth.

Permission:

I have read and understand the Disclosure (above) and the **Kid Talk** Agreement.

_____
Student's Name or Names

I give my permission for my child/ren to participate in **Kid Talk**.

starting_____at_____
Date

_____   _____
Signature of Parent/Guardian   **Date**

Image Use Authorization (Sample)

I (we) hereby authorize the use of my (our) images, quotes, and names in the publication of information about me (us) and the activities of **Kid Talk**. Such publication(s) may be designed to raise awareness about the programs or services, and/or to raise money, in-kind donations, or volunteer assistance to support **Kid Talk** programs. The publicity includes, but is not limited to:

1. Publicity in publications, such as the newsletter, brochures, and annual report.
2. Publicity in mailings, which are sent to supporters and/or to the general public.
3. Media publicity, including television, radio, and newspapers.
4. Publicity on the internet or social media.

I (we) also give permission for the use of publicity about our experience(s) with **Kid Talk** and we have declined to accept any form of compensation for these uses.

Name_____Signed_____Date_____
           (Print name)   (Signature)

Name of Minor(s)_____Date_____
                   (Print name)   (Signature)

Name of Minor(s)_____Date_____
                          (Print name)   (Signature)

Name of Minor(s)_____Date_____
                   (Print name)   (Signature)

Name of Minor's Guardian_____Signed_____
                         (Print name)   (Signature)

Best Contact Number: (____)_____-_____

Language of Grief Glossary

NOTE: To print the PDF of this glossary for the **Glossary Card Match Game**, visit www.kidtalkgrief.com/ ktbaccess. You can print on card stock, front/back or as separate cards that can be matched in a game. Once printed, *select the terms that are appropriate* for the profile of your group of children.

ACROSTIC	A poem or narrative that uses words that start with the letters of a specific word or name to describe that word or person.
AFRAID	A feeling that can be a little bit uncomfortable (anxious) or somewhat uncomfortable (worry) or extremely uncomfortable (really scared). We are naturally afraid of the unknown.
ALPHABET POEM	A poem about a specific topic or person using the letters of the alphabet to start words or the first words of a sentence.
ANGELS	Heavenly beings created by God who live in heaven and minister to humans at God's direction.
ANXIOUS	A low level of fear that can be chronic or happen over and over.
BEREAVED	Describes a person who is grieving someone who has died.
BIBLE	The sacred book of Christianity, inspired by God, to reveal God and the story of His relationship with man.
BURIAL	To place the body of the decedent (a corpse) in a coffin or casket and bury it in the ground, usually at a cemetery with a gravestone.
CANCER	A disease that doctors treat with surgery, chemotherapy, and radiation.
CASKET	A coffin or a box or chest designed to hold a body for burial in a cemetery.
CELEBRATION OF LIFE	A gathering or service to remember and honor a person who has died.
CEMETARY	A special place where bodies are buried, and you can see gravestones.
CHURCH	The family of God or the place/building where the family of God meets.
CIRCLE OF SUPPORT	People who listen to you, care about you and want to help you.
COFFIN	A casket or container for holding a dead body to be buried in a cemetery.
CONNECTING LINK	An object that reminds you of your decedent. Examples: a necklace, a watch, a pocketknife or a pizza.

Language of Grief Glossary

CORPSE   A dead body.

CREMAINS   The ashes that remain after a body is cremated.

CREMATION   The process of burning a dead body to reduce it to ashes that will fit into a small container.

CRYPT   A special container for a body to be buried in the ground.

DEAD   Not alive or living. All plants and animals die and eventually return to the soil of the earth. A dead animal (or human) does not have a heartbeat, cannot breathe, see, talk, hear, feel, eat, or poop. The body does not work anymore. It is an empty "earth suit."

DECEDENT   A dead person.

DEPRESSED/DEPRESSION   A mental condition characterized by prolonged feelings of despair and dejection. As a situational response, depression is a normal part of grieving.

ETERNAL/ETERNITY   The Christian point of view is that we are created to be eternal beings in relationship with God forever and ever. Our bodies are not eternal but our soul, spirit, mind, will and emotions are. We will have new heavenly bodies someday when we have put our faith in Jesus and received the gift of His salvation which He accomplished for us on the cross.

FIRST RESPONDERS   Firefighters, police, paramedics and/or ambulance drivers are all professionals who arrive at the scene of a 911 call to help people with a health crisis, accident or crime.

FORGIVE   A choice to let go of blame and anger when you have been hurt by someone. You may have to do it every time you remember the offense.

FUNERAL   A special service to honor the memory of someone who has died. Often the decedent is in a casket at the funeral for those who come to see in order to say good-bye. It is usually held at the funeral home or cemetery.

GOD/JESUS/HOLY SPIRIT   All are the creator and sustainer of the universe and the author of the Bible. God came to earth as Jesus and He sent the Holy Spirit to dwell among and within us and to comfort us in the here and now.

GOSPEL   The "good news" that God came to earth as Jesus to help us know Him, to demonstrate His love for us and then to suffer and die on the cross to pay the penalty for our sins. Jesus came back from death. He gives us both the gift of eternal life when we believe in Him and the privilege of being His adopted children during our time on earth.

Language of Grief Glossary

GRATEFUL

A glad and appreciative heart for events, circumstances, and things in your life. Perceiving things as a "blessing."

GRIEF

Our internal response – feelings, thoughts, and emotions – to loss and separation from anyone or anything that we value. Grief can influence our behavior so that we say and do things that are not our "normal" self.

GRIEF ATTACK

When emotions sneak up on you, but you were OK a minute ago.

GRIEF BUNDLE

The total of our grief responses to separation and loss that have been accumulating our whole lives – like a paperclip chain. Our whole grief bundle can recycle with a big emotional response – too big for the little loss that may have just happened. It will also recycle with the calendar and with sights, smells and memories. Shrinking our grief bundle is a goal of griefwork.

GRIEF VOMIT

This is when grief erupts out of your mouth when you were not expecting it. You may say things or use a tone of voice that you would not normally say if you were not grieving.

GRIEFWORK

Any activity we choose to do that helps us express the emotions of grief including the love that we still feel for the person who died.

HAPPY SNAPS

Close your eyes and visualize a "photo" moment of your decedent that makes you smile. That is a "happy snap" (shot).

HEAL

The pain of grief no longer dominates your life and you have the energy to invest in living again. It does not mean that you stop loving or forget the person who died.

HEAVEN

The eternal abode that God has prepared for us when we believe the gospel and choose to make Jesus the Lord of our lives.

HOMICIDE

The killing of one person by another.

HOSPITAL

A place where doctors, nurses and healthcare professionals work very hard to make "patients" healthy and well again.

IMPRINTS

Like a fingerprint in clay, a person may make an impression or imprint on us, especially people who are close to us. Someone may influence who we are or who we want to become. Maybe we are like them in some way or like to do the same things. Examples: love puppies or a sense of humor. Maybe they said words that we will always remember. Or maybe we would just like to make them proud of us.

Language of Grief Glossary

LAST RESPONDERS Funeral professionals who help and support the families of a decedent.

LONELY Lonely is feeling oneself to be alone and longing for company or friends. When we are grieving, we miss the person who died and wish they were here with us

MAUSOLEUM A large stately tomb or a building housing such a tomb or tombs.

MEMORIAL A special event where people gather to celebrate the life of someone important to them.

MEMORIALIZE An activity that honors or reflects love for a person or persons who died. Examples: putting flowers on the grave, lighting a candle, making a scrapbook.

MORTUARY A building where decedents are kept until burial or cremation.

MOURN To feel and/or express deep sorrow or grief. Mourning is the behaviors of grief – the way the pain of grief may come out in our actions.

MVA Motor Vehicle Accident.

RITUAL An activity or ceremony that reflects care for the person who died. It may mark special occasions or honor people or events. Examples: having a special meal of the decedents favorite foods or blowing bubbles and saying, "I love you, grandma!"

SAFE PLACE A location where a person both thinks and feels that they are safe from any kind of harm.

SALVATION Salvation for Christians is being saved from death and separation from God by Christ's death and resurrection. It means that those who believe in Him become children of God with eternal life in His presence in heaven.

STRESS Pressure, force, or strain. To be under pressure is to feel stressed.

STRESS MANAGEMENT Practices that lessen the sense of being under pressure. They include eating well, getting enough sleep, exercise, deep breathing, a gratitude list, prayer, and meditation and more.

SUICIDE When a person chooses to die by taking their own life.

TOILET BOWL LOVE When we choose to "flush" the words or behaviors that have hurt us so that we do not get "yucky" inside. A symbolic way to forgive as often as necessary.

TREASURED MEMORIES Memories of our decedents that we love to remember and do not ever want to forget.

Terms & Conditions of Use

All printables are intended for your Personal Use ONLY.

- Printables **ARE NOT** to be added to any other website or distributed in any way (this includes message boards or email list). If you wish to share my printables, send them the link to my site.

- Printables are not to be compiled and given or resold on disc or any form of printed or electronic media.

- You can only print these for Personal Use.

- You cannot copy or edit any of the graphics to create new graphics to share or sell as your own.

If you want to share the **Kid Talk** or *Our Story* printables with friends or colleagues, please do not send them copies of the the files, but send them the links to my website instead at: www.kidtalkgrief.com/ktbaccess.

You are not allowed to edit any part of my printables and graphics to create your own digital graphics unless you intend to use those graphics only for your own personal use with grieving children.

If you are a business and wish to use Kid Talk or *Our Story* printables for printed materials, please ask here: mel@kidtalkgrief.com.

Our Story

A Memory Book for

_____

_____

and

Me

AND

The Story of My Broken Heart

By

_____

_____

(date)

Our Story - Contents

Above The Surface ...
Looking Composed &
Unruffled,

Below The Surface ...
Paddling Like Crazy!

Quack!!
I'm Just Ducky!!

Image Courtesy of Freepik

Grief is Like an Onion

AN ONION . . .

YOU PEEL IT

ONE LAYER AT A TIME

AND

YOU CRY A LOT . . .

Tears Poem

Tears on the outside
Fall to the ground and
are slowly swept away.

Tears on the inside
Fall on the soul and
stay, and stay, and
stay.

Silent Hurting Heart Poem

"Oh, nothing's wrong," she smiled
and said, grinning from ear to ear.
The frown that just was on her face
seemed to disappear.

But deep down where secrets are kept,
the pain began to swell.
All the hurt inside of her
just seemed to stay and dwell.

She'd duck into the bathrooms
and hide inside the stalls,
because no one could see her tears
behind those dirty walls.

All the pain in her heart
was too much for her to take.
Pretending everything's O.K.
is much too hard to fake.

She was sick and tired of loosing
and things never turning out right.
She had no hope left in her.
She was ready to give up the fight.

She wiped away the teardrops,
put a smile back on her face,
pulled herself together, and
walked out of that place.

Life went on and things got better.
She thought that was a start.
But still no one could see inside
her silent hurting heart.

By Dayna Erickson, Seventh Grade Student, May 2, 1991

My Silent Hurting Heart

My heart is broken because_____died on _____

(Write the name.) (Write the date.)

This is my broken heart.

Grief is what I feel inside when someone I love dies. I also feel grief when I am separated from anyone or anything that is important to me. It's a lot of work putting a broken heart back together. (It's called "griefwork!") It can take a long time.

My heart will never be quite the same.

All About Me...

My name is_____. I'm in grade_____

at_____(school). I was born_____(month/day/year).

I live with_____in_____.
                         (names of people)   (city/state)

I am_____tall. I have_____hair and_____eyes.
      (feet & inches)   (your hair length & color)   (your eye color)

I like to wear_____. My favorite color is_____.

My favorite food(s) is/are:_____.

My pets are:_____.

My favorite song and/or singing group is: _____

_____.

My favorite movie is:_____.

My best friend is:_____.

At school I like:_____.

In my free time I like to:_____.

On weekends I usually:_____.

This summer I want to:_____.

Someday I want:_____.

I feel good when:_____.

Meet My_____

I will always love_____. I will never forget_____.

These are things that I will always remember about_____.
(Make a list or draw a picture.)

Eventually, if I do my griefwork, when I think of_____,

it won't hurt so much .

9

Favorite Things

Here's a list of_____**'s favorite:**

People_____

Place to visit/vacation_____

Color_____Animal _

Foods _____

Flowers/Fragrance_____

Car/Transportation_____

Free time activity_____

Sport/Team_____

Music/Music Group_____

Radio Station_____

Movie/Movie Star_____

T.V. Program_____

His/her Pet Peeve_____

Acrostic Example

D – drummer of "Wipe Out"
O – oldest child
N – nutty and fun

P – patient with baby sister

A – always played games/cards to win

U – under tall to suit his taste

L – loved to drive circles in the Bartel's car

E – eager to play basketball or baseball

R – really good friend to Lou & Aaron

I – irritated with his brother

C – courageous in battling cancer

K – kind to animals and little kids

S – sure to have the last word

O – often his dad's pal

N – nice to have around

You will always be my precious__son__.

I love you,_Donny_.   *Mom*   Nov. 14, 2000
                        (signature)   (date)

An Acrostic for _____.

Write your loved one's name in a column down the left side of this page. Then think of words or phrases that describe him or her which start with those letters.

Alphabet Poem (Sample)

About Don Paul Erickson

By Mom

A

Beloved

Child

Donny was

Every thing a parent could want in a child

Frequent talks

Genuinely likable

Had lots of enthusiasm for life

Involved in sports

Just any game with a ball

Kind to animals

Loved to be in the front of the line

Made lots of friends

Never complained about being sick

Once he ran the Sound to Narrows with Dad

Probably never kissed a girl

Quiet in his last days

Really good drummer

Small for his age

Tried hard to play well

Unfinished business of living

Valued his family & friends

Wanted to win every game

X-rays revealed the tumor

You will always be loved

Z until the end of time

Alphabet Poem

About_____

By _____

_____
(date)

A	N
B	O
C	P
D	Q
E	R
F	S
G	T
H	U
I	V
J	W
K	X
L	Y
M	Z

My Personal Experience with Death

When I think about death _____

_____

When I think about my _____ 's death, I wonder _____

_____

What makes it difficult to talk about death is _____

_____

One way my life has changed because of the death is _____

One of my favorite memories of being with my _____is

_____

At the funeral I _____

One thing I wish my teachers understood is _____

_____

I wish my friends would _____

I would like my mom and dad to know _____

The biggest change since _____ died is _____

_____

It isn't easy for me to admit _____

One of my greatest fears is _____

When I'm feeling really sad, it helps me to _____

_____

About the Death

Write what you know (or draw a picture) about how your loved one died.

Funeral/Memorial Service

For_____,

(Write his or her name.)

It was held on_____at_____.

(date)   (name of place it was held)

Who was there? Family_____.

Friends_____.

If you didn't attend, tell why_____.

What stands out in your mind about the service?

_____.

What music was played?

_____.

Who spoke?_____.

What did you like about the service?_____.

_____.

What part was hard for you?_____.

What would you change?_____.

_____was_____. His/Her_____

(Name or He/She)   (buried or cremated)   (remains or cremains)

are now located at_____. After the service

_____.

"Gone from my presence, ever present in my heart."

We Remember Them

A Responsorial Poem

At the rising of the sun and its going down
We remember them.
At the blowing of the wind and the chill of winter,
We remember them.
At the opening of the buds and the rebirth of spring,
We remember them.
At the shining of the sun and in the warmth of summer,
We remember them.
At the rustling of the leaves and in the beauty of autumn,
We remember them.
At the beginning of the year and at its end,
We remember them.
As long as we live, they too will live; for they are now a part of us, as
We remember them.
When we are weary and in need of strength,
We remember them.
When we are lost and sick at heart,
We remember them.
When we have joy we crave to share,
We remember them.
When we have decisions that are difficult to make,
We remember them.
When we have achievements that are based on theirs,
We remember them.
As long as we live, they too will live; for they are now a part of us, as
We remember them.

A Litany of Remembrance Poem by Rabbi Sylvan Kamens and Rabbi Jack Riemer.
© Central Conference of American Rabbis. Used by kind permission of the CCAR.

My Grief Bundle

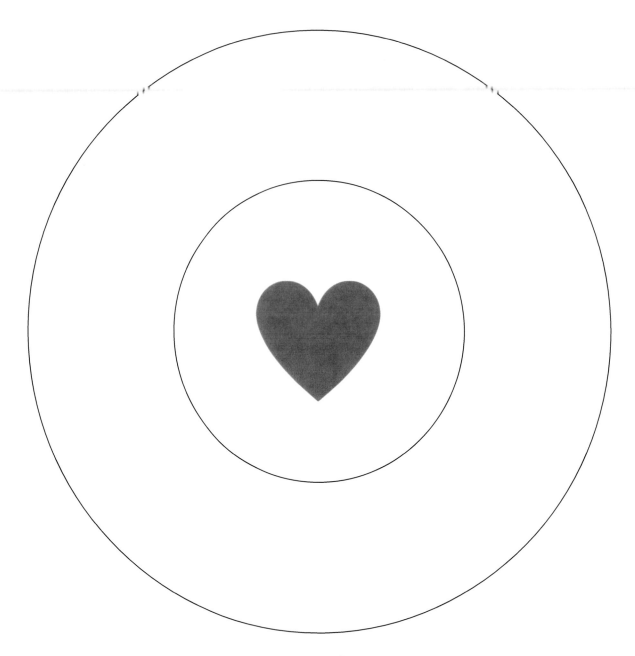

Everyone has a grief bundle of all the separations and losses experienced since birth. Here is mine. With each new loss I might feel the grief of my *whole* grief bundle. A *part* or *all* of my grief bundle may "recycle" as a "grief attack." This may explain my <u>big</u> reactions to little losses!
It will also probably recycle when I am a teenager.

My Feelings of Grief

Feelings are not right or wrong. They just **are**. I *have* to "feel" my grief in order to "heal." Here are some of my feelings.

(Write words or draw pictures or both.)

Grief can make you feel like you're going crazy.

Watermelon Hugs

Sometimes I'm sad;
I mean very-very sad.
Sometimes I'm mad;
I mean very-very mad.

Sometimes my feelings
Are in a jumbled-up way;
But my words get stuck
And I don't know what to say.

I need a secret word
That I can softly say
To let my people know
"I need some hugs today."

There's *flipper-flap* and *snipper-snap*
And *blueberry* and *baba-bee;*
But **WATERMELON** seemed just right—
It's the best secret word for me.

I shared my secret word with some
Special people--just a few---
So, when they hear **WATERMELON,**
They will know just what to do.

Now when I'm sad and want to hide
Under my fuzzy bear rug,
I just whisper **WATERMELON,**
And I get a great big HUG!

Carol Weedman Reed 2010 Printed by permission.

The Pain of Grief

Sometimes I physically feel the pain of grief. This is where and how I feel it in my body

We Will Light Candles

We Will Light Candles

Candles of joy despite all sadness

Candles of hope where despair keeps watch

Candles of courage for fears ever present

Candles of peace for tempest-tossed days

Candles of graces to ease heavy burdens

Candles of love to inspire all our living

Candles that will burn all year long

Author Unknown

Grief Behaviors

(Mourning)

Some of my grief behaviors aren't planned. Sometimes my grief behavior just "leaks" or it may come out like a volcano or "grief vomit." These actions come from a lot of jumbled up feelings. It's OK as long as I don't hurt myself or other people. These expressions of my grief are what is called "mourning."
Here are some ways I have shown my grief.

1._____

2._____

3._____

4._____

5._____

6._____

7._____

8._____

Toilet Bowl Love
(Royal Flushes)

I've written some examples of things people say and do that hurt my feelings or make me mad. I choose to flush all that.

Griefwork

To "heal" means that I will be able to remember_____without so much pain. It means that I will enjoy living again. It does **not** mean that I will forget_____or stop loving him/her.

Sometimes I will still miss him/her a lot. I will always love and remember_____. I will love others also. Griefwork is what I do that will help me work *through* the pain of grief. For example, I can:

It's not healthy to grieve all day. So, when I need a break from "griefwork," these are things that I can do to help myself feel better:

It may take a long time and be a lot of hard work that doesn't feel good, but *I choose to do things that will help me to heal.*

_____
(your signature)

26

How My Family Has Changed

Many things have changed since_____died.

     The changes I like are: The changes I don't like are:

_____   _____

_____   _____

Before_____died, my family looked like this:

Now my family looks like this:

Imprints - Your Mark on My Life

When I push my finger into clay, it leaves a mark. _____
has made a mark on my life. The parts of me that may be like him/her
are:

Things I <u>have</u> or like to <u>do</u> that are like him/her are:

Marks that I do not like and want to change about me are:

I can celebrate the good marks that_____has made on my
life. I can work at changing what I want to be different about me. I can
live so that_____would be very proud of me. This will help my
broken heart heal. I am becoming a new and unique ME.

I will always be_____'s _____
                                            (son, daughter, sister, etc.)

Dreams

The death of someone loved can make kids have bad or weird dreams. They may be scary or upsetting.
Draw a dream you can remember.

Bad dreams get better over time.
Draw or tell how you would change your dream.

My Circle of Support

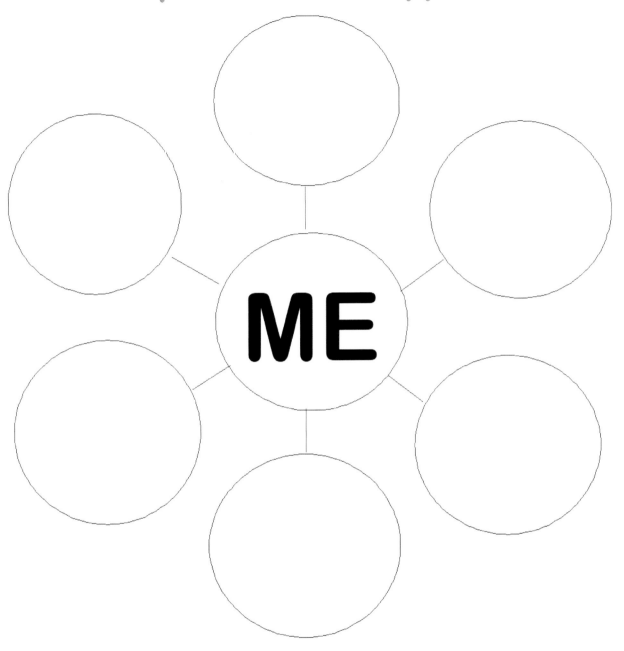

My circle of support are the people who care about me,
listen to me, and help me. Here they are.
These are the people I can talk to.

My Safe Place

Sometimes I need a quiet place where I can feel safe and be alone with my feelings. Here's a picture of my safe place.

Will I Heal?

To "heal" means that I will remember_____without hurting so much. It means that I will feel more like myself and want to do things that are fun: my life will seem good again.

To "heal" does not mean that I will forget_____or stop loving him/her. It does not mean that I won't feel the pain of grief ever again. There will always be reminders that may make me sad. Or happy. Or both.

This is a picture of me after_____died and how I will look someday when I've done my griefwork.

<u>After</u>   <u>Someday</u>

Bouquet of Memories

These are some of my favorite memories of

_____.

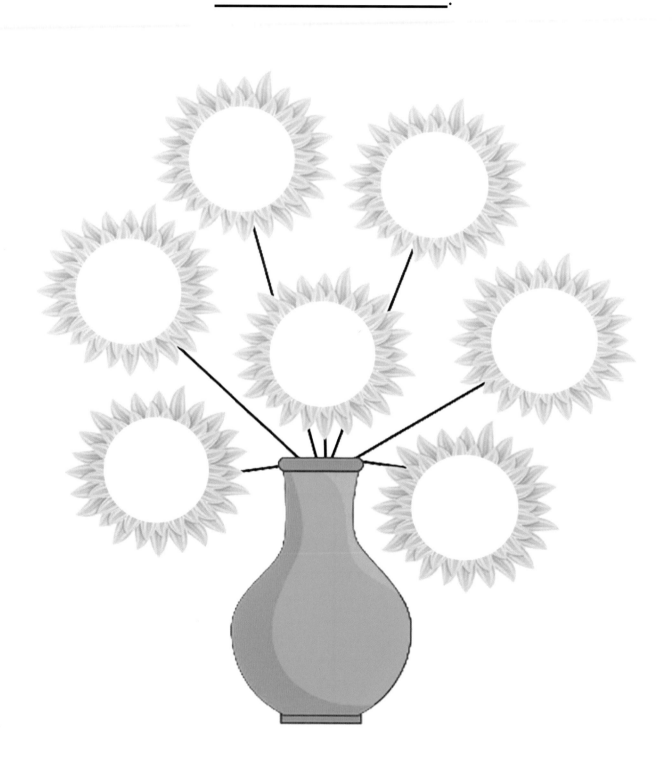

My Gratitude List

Even though I am sad when I miss_____, there are lots of things that I can be glad about. When I think about them, my heart feels lots better.

1._____

2._____

3._____

4._____

5._____

6._____

7._____

8._____

9._____

10._____

It is a healthy habit to add to my Gratitude List every day, even after my broken heart heals.

Treasured Memories

When someone we love dies, our memories of them become our treasure. Reach inside this treasure chest to find some memories about_____that I treasure.

Love You Forever...

I will always love_. These are ways that I can still show my love
for_____. (Make a list. Pick your favorite and draw a picture on the back of this page.)

1. _____

2. _____

3. _____

4. _____

5. _____

6. _____

7. _____

8. _____

9. _____

10. _____

11. _____

12. _____

A Special Letter

_____
(today's date)

Dear_____,

_____

_____

_____

_____

_____

_____

_____

_____

_____
(Your Name)

When Someone Else
Has A Broken Heart...

Sometimes I can tell that someone else has a broken heart. They look sad or mad or don't want to play or talk. They might be grieving because they had to say good-bye to someone or something that they cared about, or maybe someone died. These are ways I can be a good friend to someone who is grieving. (The pictures will give you a hint.)

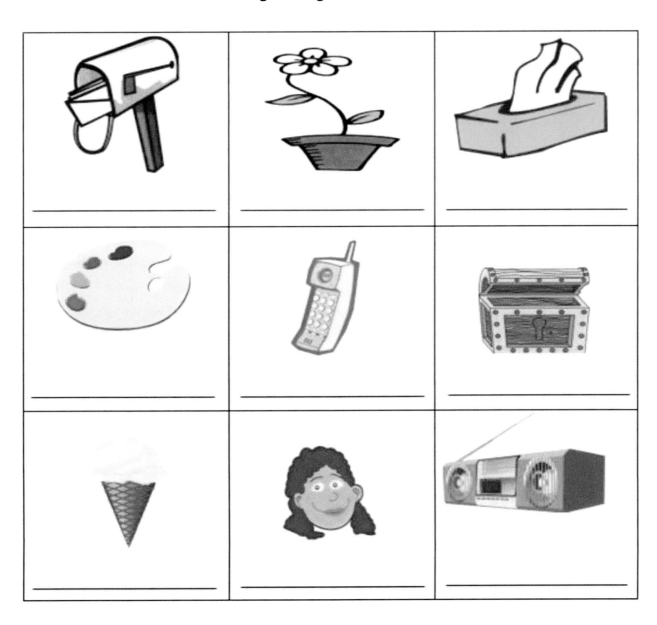

Reviews

*"I loved **Kid Talk**, because when someone you love dies, you don't really want to talk about it, but they encourage you to talk about it, and you feel a lot better."*
Sophie age 12.

* * * *

*"With the 'two-in-one' **Kid Talk** Curriculum and **Our Story Memory Book**, you have a **complete** step-by-step guide to helping grieving children, polished over thirty years. Use this proven comprehensive package to facilitate a grief support group and to help each child work through their grief by creating their personal **"Our Story"** memory book to cherish forever.*

"Having run many bereavement support groups for families; I value this curriculum because it delivers effective projects to help a child grieve in healthy ways. The book's layout covers 14 weeks of Lesson Plans with grief-specific activities, tips for facilitators, plus pages for each child to help them build their personal memory book.

"Each week has a theme, supply list, activity choices, work sheets, handouts for parents and kids, home Griefwork assignments, online resource links, and even themed snack food suggestions, that aid the normal grief process.

"In my opinion there is no better publication available than this concise, practical tool to guide you as you help grieving children." **-Nanette Flynn, MPM, CT (retired)**

* * * *

*"**Kid Talk** author, Mel Erickson has a huge heart for grieving children, evident in her Faith-based Kid-Talk **Curriculum** including the **Our Story Memory Book**. Her 13-week program draws upon her personal encounters with childhood and adult grief, and more than 30 years' work experience in the field of grief recovery support, for both adults and children.*

*"Mel has meticulously provided everything necessary for this successful program, providing children who have lost a loved one with all the tools they will need to travel their own personal grief journey. I have personally witnessed the success of **Kid-Talk**, over a number of years working with Mel on our Churches' grief recovery support team."*
-Paul Conger, Grief Recovery Support Team, Lighthouse Christian Center.

* * * *

Kid Talk & *Our Story* Memory Book – Thank You!

Thank you for your interest in helping grieving kids.

Your honest review will help others find this book on Amazon.

Was it helpful? In what way? Take a few moments and share your thoughts on this publication.

Please leave your review on Amazon.

Mel Erickson

* * * *

Newsletter Sign-Up

Would you like more tips, tools, and resources?

If yes, please sign up for our

FREE Newsletter

Grief Talk.

Sign Up At: www.kidtalkgrief.com

Keep up to date with the latest information and guidance.

When you sign-up, we will send you a FREE copy of

"*How to Break Tragic News to A Child*"

Let's chat: mel@kidtalkgrief.com or on www.kidtalkgrief.com.

I will gladly answer you.

Please visit www.kidtalkgrief.com for our full Privacy Policy and Terms of Service.

By The Same Author

12 Simple Tips and Tools to Help Your Grieving Child
What I Wish I'd Known When My Son Died

This little handbook is perfect to give to grieving caregivers who want to help a bereaved child in their life. It contains everything I hungered to know for my own kids when I was hurting after my son died.

Topics covered include:

- ✓ How to Break Bad News to a Child
- ✓ Is my Child's Grief Normal?
- ✓ How Can I Help My Grieving Child?
- ✓ Should My Child Come to the Remembrance Service?
- ✓ What Words Do I Use to Explain…

Available as a paperback book or an eBook on Amazon

Paperback - ISBN 978-7365868-3-9
eBook – ISBN 978-1-7365868-2-2

Also In The Same Series
Our Story Memory Book

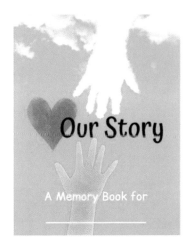

This standalone version of the *Our Story* **Memory Book** is available for larger groups of children. It is identical to the edition published with the **Kid Talk** Curriculum and is designed to work alongside the detailed program in the book.

It means facilitators can provide each child with a ready-to-go memory book from the get-go and saves time.

Available as an 8.5" x 11" full color paperback activity book from Amazon.

Part of the **Kid Talk Series**

ISBN - 978-1-7365868-1-5

Made in the USA
Coppell, TX
13 May 2025

49277434R00117